1961

CONTEMPORARY CHURCH ART

CONTEMPORARY CHURCH ART

by Anton Henze
and Theodor Filthaut

TRANSLATED BY CECILY HASTINGS
EDITED BY MAURICE LAVANOUX

SHEED & WARD : NEW YORK

This book was translated from KIRCHLICHE KUNST DER GEGENWART, published by Paulus Verlag, Recklinghausen, Germany.

Manufactured in the United States of America

CONTENTS

PREFACE TO THE GERMAN EDITION   7

PREFACE TO THE AMERICAN EDITION   9

ANTON HENZE: **The Potentialities of Modern Church Art and Its**
 Position in History   15
  Christian and Church Art in the 19th and 20th Centuries   15
  The Modern Church   20
  Painting and Sculpture in Church   27
  God's Tent among Men   32
  The Patron's Responsibility   33
  The *Instructio de arte sacra*   35
  From the Basilica to the Tent of God   37
  The Position of Modern Art in History   44
  New Possibilities   46

THEODOR FILTHAUT: **Church Art and the Liturgy**   49

  The Lord's House   49
  The Altar   53
  The Sanctuary   56
  The Font   58
  The Porch   59
  Pictures and Statues   60

ILLUSTRATIONS

  European   1- 89
  Mexican   26- 27
  United States   90-127

5

PREFACE TO THE GERMAN EDITION

THIS BOOK IS a discussion of church art today. It is not concerned with the general question of works of art with Christian themes, but with the construction of the church itself and with such pictures, statues, furnishings and vestments as may find a place within it. The examples chosen are ones which we consider legitimate, or at any rate fruitful and important. We have taken them where we found them. Our illustrations were not chosen for the perfection of their artistic achievement but for their representative qualities. The text is intended to clarify the situation and interpret the works shown. It aims at giving an answer from the history of Western art to those who ask where twentieth-century art stands. Considerable space is devoted to this, because misunderstandings of legitimate contemporary art always resort to historical arguments. On this historical survey is based a discussion of the potentialities and limitations of church art in our time, from repository trash to abstract painting.

The first essay is an attempt to deal in outline with the questions provoked, in friend and foe alike, by the ecclesiastical buildings and pictures produced by contemporary architects and artists. The second endeavours to answer those questions which are put by the artist—all too often in vain—to the Church in her rôle as patron. It outlines the theological context and the liturgical data which must be the point of departure for the building and adornment of the church.

This book has been produced in the hope that it will not only provide some much-needed guidance for patrons and artists within the Catholic Church, but also contribute to a general discussion of architecture and the visual arts in the twentieth century.

PREFACE TO THE AMERICAN EDITION

WE LIVE IN challenging times. During recent decades, since the first World War, we have lived through political upheavals in many parts of the world, and science has entered into a fascinating if somewhat frightening era. In the relatively calmer atmosphere of art there have been changes as well; in the special field of religious art we can now find evidences of life, even vigorous life.

If we look at the past in these United States we realize that the immense job of carving a living out of the land was not always conducive to the creation of beauty. In fact, in those early days of barely a century ago we relied to a great extent on European sources, and this at a time when those sources were redolent of Victorian norms; an age which, we see in retrospect, produced an art based on a misunderstanding of the great art of past ages. It was in reality a time when Americans were suffering from an inferiority complex in the realm of art. It was largely a period of artistic snobbishness, of *nouveau-riche* vulgarity bolstered up by the power of the dollar. It was an unhealthy period, and we need shed no tears over its passing. The real tragedy of that era lies in the fact that the art consciousness of our architects became haunted by a nostalgia for an imagined past, with a consequent disregard for the needs of their time. In an attempt to get rid of the type of art known as Victorian, artists and architects in the United States saw salvation in a return to an assumed purity of past glories, and in the field of religious art, this return led straight to pseudo-Gothic and pseudo-Romanesque.

Recent decades, however, have witnessed a return to sanity. But the irony of the situation is that this return to a saner outlook has not been entirely due to conviction but rather has come about through economic necessity. It has come to be increasingly difficult, if not well-nigh impossible, to plan churches loaded with the fake trappings of the past. Increased costs of construction, higher wages for labor, have forced client and designer to see a way out of the impasse through simplicity and what might be termed "pure design." But the isms of the past have been replaced by the isms and the clichés of the present to such an extent that a great deal of our architecture has now become sterile and clinical. We are now in need of the warmth that only the artist can bring into our churches.

If we look at the history of architecture through the ages we will find that each age produced a distinctive architecture of its own; informed, it is true, by ramification of design elements from far and near, but surely not on the basis of style as we have come to accept the term today. It does seem that all art and architecture, prior to the nineteenth century at

9

any rate, *was modern in its day,* and it was modern in the proper sense of that much-abused word for the simple reason that no one called it so. It was unconsciously modern; it is when we become consciously modern that our troubles begin.

The history of architecture furnishes us continual evidence that the great practitioners of past ages worked out their problems with imagination, daring, creativeness, a sense of proportion, a sense of tradition; they even risked failure, but always in a free manner and with intuition. It is true, of course, that the ancient architects were aware of much of what had been done before their day and were influenced in various ways by the work of their predecessors, but they did not slavishly copy; rather did they allow their work to evolve in a normal fashion, with due respect for the needs of their time.

In the years since the exciting days of the 1930's we have been busy finding a way out of the impasse into which we had been led by the pseudo-mediaevalists. One way to clean up the debris is to return to a consideration of the liturgy. We know that the liturgy is a task, a service, an act of homage; it is the characteristic act of religion. It is the official cult of the Church. It is a social act because it is the prayer and sacrifice offered for the salvation of mankind and which the clergy, clothed with the authority of the Church, offers publicly to God at the altar, often in the midst of a large congregation, and in the name of all for all. Many of our present difficulties can be solved by this return to first principles, to the liturgy; to art in relation to that liturgy. The liturgy has naturally developed into a work of art. It always bore within itself the seed of beauty. And so it is that the place where that liturgy is performed, the church structure, should be planned in the best possible manner and with due regard for the needs of our day; for the liturgy, like tradition, is a dynamic force, and not merely a brake on our imagination or creative faculties.

It is true that we no longer have a living tradition of art; we are faced with the difficulty of rediscovering a tradition in the midst of an active and somewhat chaotic civilization. Even so, our task is not so much to pay homage to a hollow concept of tradition as it is to seek a link with authentic tradition, and that means seeking a living art. Such a point of view implies an art based on universal values; in a way, we can say a *timeless* art.

All this is particularly true today because of the greatly accelerated tempo of life. We are faced with a challenge because we must seek the revival of the artistic climate of past ages amidst the chaotic conditions of the present, and we must also escape the tendency to fall into the extremes of self-expression. In a consideration of a truly creative art, we can and must draw a reasonable distinction between unbridled sentimentalism and all that is purely idiosyncratic in the art of our day, and that which represents an honest and legitimate effort to make all the arts more effective in the service of the Church.

We cannot entirely escape some kind of antiquarian retrospection and certain national

10

traits may incline us towards indulgence for the glories of art still to be seen in the lands of our forebears. That is only natural. What, however, is not natural, is to indulge to excess in this nostalgic speculation, or to become involved in the fantasy of dreams of the past. And if we are really sentimental about it, we can fall into the delusion of assuming that the prospect of another life which we might have lived would be preferable to that in which we live here and now. That was the trap into which the proponents of a supposed Gothic revival fell some fifty years ago.

The confusion which reigns today and stiffens the resistance of the die-hard is due in large measure to our having, so to speak, reached the bottom of the barrel, as far as design is concerned. The past twenty-five years have witnessed the gradual disappearance of meaningless ornament and false trappings based on antiquarian mistakes. In church work, these mistakes took the form of plaster vaults and fake buttresses, revolting statuary and insipid paintings. But today we are coming close to the obliteration of art with the excessive use of glass and aluminum, the *total* elimination of mouldings, etc; the engineer is disturbingly in the ascendent, the artist is feared, and many architects are reluctant to take the responsibility of employing great artists, or even to run the risk of apparent failure. We have reached a point where *pure* design reigns supreme, to the extent of sterility. The danger now lies in the fact that certain clichés of the present may take the place of the imitations of recent decades. The architects who liberated us from the shackles of past aberrations have now acquired their imitators among those who chronically imitate—owing to lack of ability, timidity and want of conviction—and never themselves invent. They are the sad army of "cafeteria" architects—those who will give the public what it wants, regardless.

What we sorely need today, in the field of religious art and architecture, is the realization that man is not only a creature of intellect but also one of emotion; he cannot be reduced to the level of a thinking machine. In the design and decoration of our churches we must add the warmth that comes from the artist's work—the painter, the sculptor, the ceramist, the enamelist, the stained-glass worker, the iron worker, the silversmith, the worker in textiles, the calligrapher, the printer, all working in close collaboration with the architect. How all this can be done is the problem of our day.

As if life was not difficult enough as it is, a normal evolution of religious art is choked off and obstructed by the semantic battle which fogs all official pronouncements, to say nothing of the commentaries of many whom the mere hint of a fresh idea calls to do battle with fate. It is such a useless battle! Instead of inveighing against the hopes of artists who wish for nothing more than to devote their God-given talents to the creation of that beauty which we all wish to see in the House of God, it might be wiser to concentrate our efforts on the elimi-

11

nation of the trash that clutters so many of our churches and which is still sold in such quantities. The efforts of many artists who are labelled "modern" (and what a bugbear that word has become!) have not even been given a chance to validate the claims of architects and artists who stand ready to work for a renewal of that artistic climate which must be a prelude to a sane outlook in matters of religious art. But seldom do we hear any official outcry against the continuance of a regime of commercialism that can only be called a prostitution of all we hold dear in manifestations of beauty on earth.

We cannot eliminate human nature from this problem, but we can clarify the issues by an appeal to the *magisterium* of the Church, and in the matter of art this leads us to the short passages in Pope Pius XII's encyclical *Mediator Dei:*

... Recent works of art which lend themselves to the materials of modern composition, should not be universally despised and rejected through prejudice. Modern art should be given free scope in the due and reverent service of the church and the sacred rites, provided that they preserve a correct balance between styles tending neither to extreme realism nor to excessive "symbolism," and that the needs of the Christian community are taken into consideration, rather than the particular taste or talent of the individual artist. Thus modern art will be able to join its voice to that wonderful choir of praise to which have contributed, in honor of the Catholic faith, the greatest artists throughout the centuries. Nevertheless, in keeping with the duties of Our office, We cannot help deploring and condemning those works of art, recently introduced by some, which seem to be a distortion and perversion of true art and which at times openly shock Christian taste, modesty and devotion, and shamefully offend true religious sense. These must be entirely excluded and banished from our churches, like anything else that is not in keeping with the sanctity of the place.

This encyclical is addressed to "The Venerable Brethren the Patriarchs, Primates, Archbishops, Bishops and other Ordinaries in Peace and Communion with the Apostolic See," and so the bishops throughout the Catholic world are charged with the operation of these general directives. And since it is a province in which all of us feel a vested interest, it is only natural that personal interpretation should lead to confusion based on prejudice, valid or otherwise. It has been remarked by some, who would wish the Holy See to legislate in a strict manner on matters connected with the religious arts, that the papal words in this encyclical were in the main of negative value, since in reality the positive pronouncements were practically cancelled out by the prohibitions. Such an interpretation fails to recognize the generosity of the Holy See in questions that do not easily allow for direct legislation. It is true that the Holy Father allows for a modern point of view in matters of art and architecture, then follows this up by the inevitable "nevertheless" and an appeal to tradition. But the wisdom of the Holy See is quite clear to any who can understand and freely accept the authority of the Church, *qua* authority. There is here no misunderstanding. If, as the catechism tells us, we are created in the image and likeness of God, then the faculties and talents which the Creator has bestowed on some of us must not be thwarted or stifled by personal prejudices, individual tastes or ignorance, invincible or otherwise. As artists, we must accept the responsibility for our actions, but it remains true that those whose responsibility it is to provide the fabric in which the liturgy will be performed in all its majesty and dignity, and who are further charged with the responsibility of bringing beauty into our churches, are also bound to act in such a way that the talent bestowed by God may be not wasted or hindered through ignorance or prejudice.

The artists are legion who wish to work for the Church and within the discipline implied by the Holy Father's generous directives in *Mediator Dei*. The time is at hand for a vigorous renewal of the creative manifestations of our time. It remains for us all to make that renewal possible for the greater glory of God.

MAURICE LAVANOUX

13

ANTON HENZE

The Potentialities of Modern Church Art
and Its Position in History

CHRISTIAN AND CHURCH ART IN THE 19th AND 20th CENTURIES

CHURCH ART TODAY—as at any other period—works with the forms, colours and materials of contemporary style. Its history, like that of modern art in general, begins in the nineteenth century.

The art of the early nineteenth century is still lit by gleams of the greatness and coherence of Baroque. Hence there is still to be found, in the houses and cities of the classical style and in Biedermeier interiors, a certain seemliness and intuitive sense of rightness. This gives place to an "historicism" in which sentiment runs riot. Its building is of all styles— Romanesque and Gothic, Renaissance and Baroque. Country houses and town halls, theatres and museums, parliamentary buildings and post offices appear in shapes borrowed by the architect from the arsenal of Western history. The painter's sphere is the depiction of history and ideas. Delicate colouring and high-flown idealism go into his presentation of great historic events. Under the inspiration of Winkelmann's notions of Hellenic serenity, simplicity, nobility and grandeur, the sculptor devotes his energies to the heroes of the past. In the service of princes and the bourgeoisie art is marked by a tendency to theatricalism, showiness, alluring deception and historical illusion. In the objects soon to be mass-produced for the century's swelling masses, it all collapses into falsity and superficial sensuousness; the triumphal progress of trash begins.

But however much the historicist architect might suppose that Gothic and Baroque were the order of the day, the century had other achievements. The growth of trade called for World Exhibition buildings and up-to-date stores; new forms of transport demanded railway bridges and stations; industry developed workshops, factories and offices; the new towns required homes and places of entertainment and assembly for the growing masses of the people. Such buildings could not be constructed in traditionalist shapes and traditional materials. Iron and steel, glass and concrete took their places beside older building materials.

New technical discoveries helped to break them in. The architectural engineer constructed functional buildings out of them where historicism could find no entry; unpretentious work, developing once again from the interior outwards, it provided the elements of a new architecture.

The historical painter might like to think that he represented the supreme achievement of the age, but something still remained to spring up in the shadow of his vast canvases. The Realist movement developed its precise, unrhetorical portrayal of particular fact, and enriched it with the distress and resignation of the poor. The Naturalists caught tree and ploughland, accurate to the last dewdrop, in their painted documentaries. With swift brush-strokes of colour, the Impressionists strove to capture the light and atmosphere of the passing moment, and with it the authentic experience of the century's end. Genuinely contemporary painting and genuinely contemporary architecture came together in Germany's "Jugendstil," the New Style of the 1900's. The engineer's plain, blunt constructions began to be transformed by the architect. What had been begun by Olbrich in Darmstadt and Wagner in Vienna was carried on by men like Behrens and Pelzig. The architectural school at Chicago developed the skyscraper into a valid architectural form. In Weimar, Van der Velde turned his attention to the design of the small things of life which we handle. The German *Werkbund* provided a wider foundation for the artistic shaping of our environment. After the first World War, these stirrings of activity took shape in the *stijl* group in Holland, the Bauhaus in Germany, the ateliers of Le Corbusier and the associates of Frank Lloyd Wright.

The art of painting was reaching out to the limits and down to the primitive depths of the psyche in Expressionism; exploring the byways of Magism; and finally resolving itself into the pure symbols and coloured graphs of abstract painting. Sculpture developed on similar lines: the flowing, impressionist figures of Rodin and Rosso gave place to the solidified ideas of Moore, Marini and Heiliger, and these again to the stark symbols of Bill, Hartung and Calder. The preliminary results of this development are before us today: buildings and groups of buildings with an easy fluency of plan and transparent walls, uniting function and form in a higher architectural unity and restoring to painting and sculpture their old place in the building itself and its extension in garden or square.

During this century and a half of development in art, whose complicated course we have sketched in these few lines, what was happening to church art and Christian art? Nineteenth-century churches were under the sway of historicism and trash. There may already have been discerning spirits who recognised them as "instruments of the Father of Lies" (Egenter); reactions against them soon developed. The first half of the century saw the Nazarene movement trying to create a new school of Christian painting within a sincere, deeply-felt, idealising naturalism. It influenced the French romantics and the English Pre-Raphaelites, but in the end it mingled with the turgid waters of historicism. In the second half of the century, the

16

Beuron school aimed at a kind of ecclesiastical art in which rigid stylisation and conformity, where the human form was concerned, to a geometrical canon, was intended to produce an impersonal, liturgical spirituality. It had the right goal in view, but its deliberate reaching back to Byzantine and Egyptian art swept it, in the end, into the track of the ubiquitous contemporary historicism. Its master, Father Desiderius Lenz, had more influence as a theorist than as a painter. His ideas were an encouragement to the liturgical movement, and his aesthetic theory found congenial ground to fall on in the Nabi circle in France. Paul Serusier tried to fathom the mystery of "absolute beauty" and the "rhythm of divinity" through the "holiness of mass"; through him the influence spread to the *art sacré* movement and to Cubism. It goes without saying that Christian themes found their place in the great painting of the period. The masters of Naturalism, Realism and Impressionism all in their different ways, produced representations of Christ and the saints. The result was indubitably art of a high quality. No place was found for it within the church. Looking back at it, one hesitates to classify it as Christian art.

This poses the question of what is Christian art. Is there such a thing? There is no uniform answer. According to one point of view, all the art of Christian countries, without distinction, is counted as Christian art. Another rejects the whole concept, and simply recognises the existence of Christian themes in art and of Christians who are artists. Neither theology nor history can provide any definite answer to our question. In the past history of the West, the presence of Christian art was taken for granted whenever artists and sculptors were representing Christian themes and architects were producing buildings for a Christian purpose.

Do we still share this point of view? Do we hold that any picture or statue with a Christian theme is automatically Christian art? Obviously not, since there are some pictures whose content has a Christian source and which are self-evidently not genuine Christian art. We mean caricatures of holy persons and events, such as can be found in Roman art and among some nineteenth-century artists. We can be equally unambiguous in excluding trash, since no lie can be an expression of Christianity. A Christian work of art presupposes a legitimate artist, and the intention and desire on his part of taking his theme seriously. There were painters in the Naturalist and Impressionist schools who were real artists and who took their Christian themes seriously. Nevertheless, we are of the opinion that their works cannot be described as Christian art. There is a kind of art which is radically incapable of religious expression; and Realism, Naturalism and Impressionism belong to it.

The case is altered when we come to Symbolism and Expressionism. "No longer seeking to obtain mastery of *things*, the painter's eyes became tools for projecting an interior landscape" (Ortega y Gasset). The soul, and the realm of metaphysics to which it has access, lie open to art once more. Considerable interest is being taken in Christian themes, and the

17

best painters are devoting their energies to them. Are their works unquestionably Christian art?

The *Instructio de arte sacra,* to which we shall return again later, requires amongst other things that the man who produces a Christian work of art shall be a Christian. About the same time as it appeared, the Kestner-Gesellschaft in Hanover arranged an exhibition of Christian art in the twentieth century, in connection with the Lutheran world congress. It was not entitled "Contemporary Christian Art" but "The Christian Content in Modern Art." The assumption is implied that not every picture with a Christian theme is a Christian work of art. The catalogue stated that the sponsors of the exhibition ranked as Christian pictures only such works as had been produced by artists who were Christians working on Christian themes. This was the standard accepted by past centuries in the West. Past history and the general opinion of Christians today are at one, on this question, with the latest instruction from Rome.

There are, however, facts which seem to contradict this stipulation. Two Christian archaeologists, Kirschbaum and Hertling, affirm in their *Die römischen Katakomben* (Vienna, 1950) that early works of art, Christian in theme, were the creation of pagan artists. In our own day, the church of Assy in the French Alps provides a similar example. These facts do not by themselves settle the question of the need for Christian and artist to meet in one man. For the question still remains, whether the result was really Christian art. On the other hand, when we are dealing with artists of considerable stature we should do well to consider whether there are not borderline cases where the heights of beauty coalesce with the heights of truth. We might remember the old concept of the *anima naturaliter christiana;* those who are actually *opposed* to Christianity are hardly likely to consider devoting themselves seriously to Christian themes. Nor, finally, can any discussion of this problem overlook the truth that the artist does not work exclusively at the rational level. In creating his work, he may become "the channel and tool of higher powers." He may, as an artist, attain to levels of reality to which, as a man, in his everyday life, he remains indifferent.

However, it remains true that pictures and other works of modern art which, taking this point of view into account, are certainly Christian have been given practically no place in the Church. If we want the reasons for this, we cannot stop short at the current lack of understanding of modern art. We must realise that Christian art is not identical with church art.

Church art consists of those things which are made directly for use in the cult. The church itself and the liturgical vessels and vestments can be accepted without hesitation as church art, since they are exclusively for cult-use. It is, on the other hand, difficult to apply the

18

distinction to pictures and statues. Christian pictures and statues have a place in the church, in the cemetery, in the home and in the street.

Does an image in a church have the same significance and standing as an image in a house or beside a road? A glance at the Church's attitude towards images provides no answer. Since the iconoclast controversy, the Church has not regarded images only as a form of religious instruction; they are also to be reverenced, with a reverence which does not apply to the image itself but to that which it represents. This applies equally to images in church, by the roadside and in the home.

We will seek an answer from iconography and the Church itself. Here we find that images take their place in a certain hierarchy according to their themes. This, and the practice of the early ages in the West and the high Middle Ages, provide a basis today for the grading of images in church according to a liturgical hierarchy. It is obvious that, as our liturgical text requires, the sanctuary shall be reserved for the image of Christ. Other parts of the church may be devoted to the prophets, the apostles and the Mother of God; others again to images corresponding to particular personal devotion. This is where Christian art in general finds its way into the church, being differentiated from church art in the same way as private prayer is differentiated from the liturgy.

The distinction is primarily a matter of iconography and of the setting in which an image is placed. If we are to apply it to style as well, then what we should require of an ecclesiastical image would be a certain disciplined, symbolic, monumental quality, sacrificing individuality to objectivity. The ecclesiastical, as opposed to the Christian, image would then not be "free art," but the fulfilment of a specific task; not only would the theme be laid down, but the work would be subordinated to the purposes and requirements of its allotted place within the church.

There are twentieth-century painters and sculptors who have produced altars and statues in which these requirements are fulfilled. Only in a few exceptional cases have they found their way into the Church. This is not only the result of a misunderstanding of modern art. The real point is that there is no place for them in modern ecclesiastical architecture. If this is regarded as unfortunate or even alarming, it would be well to remember that the Church has no real need of images; the cult-image, in its primary sense, is something altogether alien to her. Images are in no way indispensable to her cult. The liturgy requires a place, an altar, a book, liturgical vessels and vestments, but not an image. In pagan antiquity, divinity—bodily and anthropomorphic—required an image conformable to the human body for its fulfilment. What the art of the Church has to do, on the other hand, is to furnish a *sign* of the infinite God: not a cult-image to *be* the god, nor a visual fulfilment of God, but a reminder of Him. In Christianity, images have lost their old central position;

19

in early Christian times, and in the early and high Middle Ages, they did not appear on the altar, but as reliquaries, and on the walls of the church; nor, even there, as individual physical entities but as parts of the "artistic whole" of the basilica, the royal church or the cathedral. Their return to the altars has coincided with a gradual loss by the Christian religion of its full significance and reality in the life of Western man.

THE MODERN CHURCH

The starting-point of architecture is man; it is a medium which gives form and emphasis to his relationships with his fellow-man, to the social forms he gives to those relationships, and to the relationship of them all to God. It gives rise to a fruitful interaction: the cause of architectonic enterprise lies in society itself; then, once it has taken shape, it in turn reaffirms and strengthens the basic forms of society and helps them to self-realisation. New architectonic forms correspond to new developments in human society.

It may be regarded as something inevitable and self-evident that the longed-for renewal of church art was bound to begin in the field of architecture, and equally self-evident that the new church architecture was not merely the result of the new styles and materials of the twentieth century. We must look for its causes rather in certain new movements in the Church which began in the nineteenth century. That century, so near to us and yet so unknown, stripped the Church of her "veil of art and showed that holy Body for the first time in all her material nakedness" (Claudel); but it also gave her fresh impulses of renewal. Theology devoted itself especially to the mystery of the Eucharist. In the various houses of the old Orders there was a recrudescence of strength, while new Orders appeared in amazing numbers: of the forty-two Orders and Congregations in Germany in 1955, no less than twenty-one were founded in the nineteenth century. From the theologians and the religious houses the new wave of life spread out to the parishes: the liturgical movement began. Its first form was given it by the work of Abbot Guéranger of Solesmes (+1875) and the revival of the chant. Pope Pius X gave it strong encouragement. It found wider scope in the efforts towards a popular liturgy made by the monasteries of Beuron, Maria Laach, Klosterneuburg and Seckau. In the Netherlands and Belgium the liturgical apostolate began. In Italy, Catholic Action developed strong liturgical features. In France, the movement was given a focal point by the Dominicans, in the United States by the periodicals *Worship* and *Amen*.

The aim of the liturgical movement was to transform the faithful from "silent onlookers" (Pius XI) to active participators in the offering; the individual worshippers were to join with the priest to form one community united by the sacrifice. It was the task of church architecture to conform to this developing community of the altar, confirming and strength-

20

ening it and providing it with an environment in which each person should be in contact with each, and all with the altar, participating visually and orally, unhindered, in the sacrifice of the Mass.

There was a long wait before the liturgical parish achieved the self-realisation of a new kind of church. Liturgy and architecture had first to make mental contact with each other and clarify their mutual relationship. Practice and theory were each dependent upon the other, finally coalescing in such a way as to make it impossible for the historian to distinguish clearly between the different contributions to the common work. In Switzerland, the painter Alexandre Cingria of Geneva flung his passionate manifesto on "The Decline of Ecclesiastical Art" into the debate. Coinciding with this came the redecoration of a small suburban church in a simple modern style. Then the nucleus was formed of the Swiss "Societas S. Lucae," so productive of future results. There were important repercussions to Cingria in France, too. Paul Claudel aligned himself explicitly with his principles and conclusions, hoping that "the estrangement between the dogmas of the faith and the artist's private world would be overcome by this approach at the level of causes and basic types." Maritain wrote *Art and Scholasticism*. Starting from the liturgical movement, the French Dominicans arrived at a new ecclesiastical art; they had an organ in *L'Art Sacré*, the discussions in which were later gathered by Father Pie Régamey in his *Art sacré au XXe siècle*. In Germany, interest in the relationship between liturgy and art was strong in the Catholic youth movement, and Romano Guardini made important contributions to the subject in lectures and writings. These German aspirations were given official formulation in the directive on "Church Planning according to the Spirit of the Roman Liturgy," prepared by T. Klauser for the liturgical commission of the Bishops' Conference at Fulda in 1947. It was followed in 1952, in France, by the "Directive of the Episcopal Commission on Pastoral Work, Liturgy and Sacred Art"; this, in accordance with the situation in France, was more concerned with modern pictures and statues in church.

It was soon clear, to theologians and architects alike, that churches which were to be the setting of the new liturgical parishes could not be constructed according to any historicist pattern. The plan, the elevation and the details of the cathedrals and Baroque churches to which historicism clings form a pattern which corresponds to another kind of liturgy and another kind of social order. To have imitated them would have meant to fail in architecture's first duty; instead of helping these new communities to self-realisation, it would have meant hindering them from reaching their true form in the liturgy. Hence we see a good deal of building still making use of historicising forms but presenting features, in the plan and the interior, which suggest the beginnings of a new kind of church. Its evolution began with Notre Dame du Raincy, built in 1923 by Auguste Perret in that district of Paris which

21

was later to see the beginnings of the priest-worker experiment. It represented the long-awaited coalescence of ecclesiastical architecture with modern architecture in its general development. It is made of glass and concrete. This, however, is not what makes it so significant: Baudot had already used steel and concrete for St. Jean de Montmartre in 1894, and Theodor Fischer for the garrison church at Ulm in 1908. What Notre Dame du Raincy shows is a new conception. In plan, it harks back to the long rectangle of the basilica, but it has compressed it and eliminated the separate choir. The altar, on its high flight of steps, retains something of the idea of the "high choir," but it has come nearer to the congregation. The pillars supporting the slightly arched roof have shrunk away to slender rods; the walls have dissolved into a honeycomb of cement, forming a gleaming pattern of coloured glass. The whole interior is light and open. Today we can look on it as an inspired forerunner of the modern twentieth-century church.

Notre Dame du Raincy was followed by churches in Switzerland and Germany which developed and clarified its new type of interior. St. Antony's at Bâle (Basel), built in 1927 by Karl Moser, looks at first sight almost like a repetition of Notre Dame du Raincy. But here we have heavier and more emphatic forms; the pillars have become square piers; the arched roof over the nave consists of deep rectangular panels, and the side-aisles, instead of the slight barrel-vaulting used at Raincy, have uncompromising, flat, deep-panelled ceilings. The walls are solid surfaces again, the glass honey-combs have become window-frames. It is behind the altar, particularly, that the solid wall comes into its own again. At Raincy, the altar seems to float in a translucent cell of its own; at Bâle, it stands firmly in front of a solidly accentuated wall. This has the effect of bringing it down to ground-level; though it is still within its own enclosure, reminiscent of the choir as it used to be, it forms part of the same spatial unit as the congregation. The unbroken wall behind the altar gives visual emphasis to this spatial unity. And whereas the exterior of Notre Dame du Raincy indulges a private whim for ornamental Gothic, St. Antony's stands in its terrace of houses simply displaying, in the architecture appropriate to concrete construction, the forms which naturally arise from its interior plan. This architectonic identity between the interior and the exterior of this church, together with its new treatment of the altar, constitute its special contribution to the future development in our times of the house of God.

When we come to Rudolf Schwarz's Church of the Blessed Sacrament at Aachen, built in 1930, both features seem already to be taken for granted. Schwarz makes no use of a separate enclosure for the altar nor of supporting pillars. One undivided space embraces both altar and congregation; yet the altar remains a little aloof from the congregation, with that remoteness which must exist between the sacred goal itself and the road to it. The

22

walls, cool and austere, enclose a long interior space. It is lit by a row of windows just under the flat roof. Thus, while it is full of bright light, it is a completely enclosed space and wholly concentrated upon the altar. The left-hand wall is pierced by a group of windows shedding the emphasis of their brighter light upon the altar, which stands in front of an unbroken wall. The interior has no pictorial or ornamental decoration whatever. Its high architectonic qualities are solely a matter of mass and proportion. It rings true throughout. Architecture has come into a proper correspondence with the liturgical congregation. Everything which is not directly concerned with the Mass has been relegated by Schwarz to a subsidiary hall at the side or to the entrance hall.

All these three churches are built on the plan of the long, aisled church. This is basically in conflict with the aim of modern ecclesiastical architecture, which is to put altar and congregation in touch with each other. So it is not to be wondered at that architects soon resorted to other types of plan. Oval and circular churches seemed particularly appropriate to the new idea. In 1932 Dominikus Böhm built the Church of St. Engelbert in Riehl (Cologne) on a circular plan. The construction makes significant use of variations on the circle-theme: four bays built on arcs of the same circle, their sections almost elliptical, combine to give the interior the effect of a mighty tent of concrete; as in Böhm's earlier church at Frielingsdorf, the dome begins at ground-level. Both in plan and in construction, the interior achieves an extraordinary degree of concentration. This is not, indeed, realised as fully as it might be, because even in these days of liturgical renewal the Church does not sanction a central position for the altar. Böhm focusses the interior upon an altar-niche; the effect of concentration is an openness toward God—such as Christian churches built for sacrifice have always had.

Notre Dame du Raincy in Paris, St. Antony's in Bâle, the Church of the Blessed Sacrament at Aachen and St. Engelbert in Cologne form between them the cradle of modern ecclesiastical architecture. Architecture is still working on the basic liturgical features of their interiors and the forms to which they gave rise. All that has been built in succeeding decades, and is now gaining ground in Europe and America as the ecclesiastical architecture of our day, has developed upon the foundations laid in these four churches, between 1923 and 1933, by Perret, Moser, Schwarz and Böhm.

A survey of the ground-plans used in modern ecclesiastical architecture shows how circle and rectangle have been combined in intermediate variants which seem better to serve the purpose of giving the altar its rightful place. Alfons Leitl has placed the altar of the Church of St. Sebastian in Aachen in the long side of the rectangle. Emil Steffan (the Franciscan Church in Cologne and St. Boniface at Dortmund), Henri Matisse (Vence) and Max Clemens von Hausen (plan for a Church in a non-Catholic district) place it at the junction between the part of the church meant for week-day use, or some similar subsidiary area, and the main part of the interior. Fritz Schaller, in the parish church at Rath (Cologne), approximates to a square plan. Dominikus Böhm displays the same tendency in the Church of Mary Queen of Peace in Cologne.

Other architects have introduced variations on the old rectangular shape. Reinhard Hofbauer, in St. Canisius in Berlin, makes the side-walls converge, ladder-like, towards the altar; Hans Schädel's St. Alphonsus in Würzburg and M. Frisac's Dominican church in Valladolid carry out the same conception. Barry Byrne has made use of two long rectangles converging and uniting, fan-like, at the altar of his Church of St. Peter and Paul in Pierre, South Dakota. In Villagio S. Francesco, Picarelli has broken up the contours on cubist lines, and achieved an extraordinary effect of concentration on a rectangular basis. At Ronchamp, Le Corbusier has taken advantage of the free, flowing lines of open-plan design to make the altar the supreme pivotal point of the whole interior.

The perfect circle, used by Böhm as the basis of his plan for St. Engelbert's, was adopted by L. G. Daneri for San Marcelino in Genoa. Instead of Böhm's concrete tent, he organises convex and concave niches into a cylindrical interior. The plain circle seems to have won most of its adherents in the Latin countries. Thus it has made its mark again, in recent years, in San Luis Gonzaga in Guadalajara, Mexico, by Enrique de la Mora y Palomar, and in the Dominican church in Sao Paulo by Sergio Bernardos. Fritz Metzger, on the other hand, for SS. Felix and Regula at Zürich, has drawn it out into a wide oval, opening smoothly into a rectangular sanctuary; Horst Linde has carried out a similar idea in the Church of the Holy Ghost, Freiburg University. For St. Albert's, Saarbrücken, Gottfried Böhm uses the circle with only a slight flattening; he gives it its orientation by strongly emphasising the altar and placing it asymmetrically, its circular base providing the tension of an echo and response to the circular basis of the tower. The plan of Paul Schneider-Eisleben's Church of St. Roch in Düsseldorf consists of segments of three overlapping circles, with the centre crowned by a three-membered dome; the altar stands in its obviously right place in the eastern segment.

There have been some fine and harmonious plans produced by the inter-penetration of circle and triangle. Kleinbeubach, by Hans Schädel, All Saints in Frankfurt, by Giefer and Mäckler, the Desert Church at Wazan, and in particular Marcel Breuer's plan for the Benedictine Abbey of St. John in Collegeville, U.S.A., are based on gentle ellipses, approximating on each side to a triangle. In Hans Schilling's Church of the Holy Angels at Wesel, Rudolf Schwarz's St. Michael's at Frankfurt, Fritz Metzger's Church of St. Francis at Riehen near Bâle and Richard Jörg's Church of the Holy Cross at Mainz, striking new patterns have been achieved from circular and triangular elements.

24

This diversity in plan is matched by a fertile diversity of construction. There is a greater and greater correspondence and unity, in these churches, between plan, section and silhouette—that unity which is the source of real greatness in architecture. This is particularly striking in the pilgrims' church of Notre Dame de la Haute at Ronchamp (1955), Le Corbusier's first church. The sweeping curves of the plan—no geometrical shapes, whether square or circular, here—are echoed both in the interior, where not only circles and right-angles but even horizontal and perpendicular planes are eschewed, and finally in the exterior, at once daring and convincing in its variations on the themes within.

Walls and roofs, like the plan itself, are naturally determined by the liturgical requirements of the congregation. Here the aim is to achieve an unconstrained and yet inescapable concentration upon the altar. The greatest contribution is made by the shape of the roof and the windows. In Fritz Metzger's Church of Our Lady of Lourdes in Zürich, the windows are circular and set under the junction of roof and walls. Their circular shape is taken up and emphasised by the transverse barrel-vaulting of which the roof consists. This leads the eye on, step by step, to the wall behind the altar, where the rhythmic sequence of circle-forms finds its goal and fulfilment in the circular setting of the picture of the Mother of God. There is another way of concentrating the windows on the altar which Metzger has also developed (there is already a suggestion of it in Schwarz's Church of the Blessed Sacrament at Aachen): a continuous strip of window running immediately under a flat roof. He gave it its earliest form in the Church of St. Charles Borromeo in Lucerne (1933), and brought it to simple perfection in SS. Felix and Regula in Zürich. A plain line of steel or wooden girders, too, arranged as they are in Lüneberg's Church of Our Lady in Gremberg (Cologne), Josef Schütz's Church of Our Lady in Solothurn, or Burlage and Niebuer's Church of St. Joseph in Greven, can serve to lead the eye forward stage by stage to the altar.

The trend towards flexible, open planning has brought a certain mobility into the roof. In St. Canisius in Berlin, by Hofbauer, it consists of half-domes of concrete of unequal heights: the space between the halves is filled in with a strip of window. This roof does not only lead the eye towards the altar: the indirect lighting from it also has the effect of gathering together and concentrating the interior. M. Frisac has adopted a similar procedure in the Dominican church in Valladolid: he has made the roof rise steeply, in steps, from the entrance to the wall behind the altar: the eye is led not only *towards* the altar but *up* to it. Hans Schädel achieves the same thing in St. Alphonsus, Würzburg, in a particularly striking fashion, by means of a plain sloping roof whose effect is heightened by the narrow strip of window running immediately under it.

Another way of emphasising the altar has been used by Giefer and Mäckler at Frankfurt

25

and Gottfried Böhm at Saarbrücken: they have heightened its visual effect by surmounting it with a glass dome, with pillars suggesting something of the protective strength of an ancient ciborium-canopy. In St. Boniface at Lübeck, Emil Steffan has placed the altar in front of a plain wall and surrounded it with an elliptical strip of window; a way of conferring on a poor church in a non-Catholic district the costly effect of a gloriole.

The effect of light in moulding the whole shape of the interior has to be considered in connection with the artificial lighting of churches. Architectonically, lamps which only light up the lower part of the interior may be a failure. The aim of artificial light should rather be to illuminate the interior in the same way as daylight. Rudolf Schwarz showed the way to a solution of this problem in the Church of the Blessed Sacrament at Aachen: there we have a series of parallel horizontal incandescent tubes, suspended from the roof at short intervals, which light up the whole of the interior. Schädel, Steffan and Baur have tried to find solutions for the as yet unsolved problem (artistically speaking) of electric light so as to form, at the same time, an integral part of the plastic adornment of the interior. But in all such attempts, the artificial lighting assumes such significance in its own right as to diminish the interior as a whole. A more practical solution might consist in strip-lighting, flush with the walls, and running parallel to the windows so as to correspond both in direction and in intensity to ordinary daylight. There are indications of such a solution in Villagio S. Francesco near Rome.

This constructional and visual concentration on the altar needs to be reinforced and completed at the level of acoustics. Architects and builders are aiming at churches in which the priest at the altar will be clearly audible, without any auxiliary apparatus, in the furthest bench at the back. The pulpit is directly related to the altar, and the organ placed near it.

These modern churches enjoy a greater freedom than other ones in their relation to their environment. There is a sense of life and movement in the way their flights of steps and subsidiary chapels, and especially their slender towers, set entirely apart from the church itself, reach out into their surroundings. Churches built on these lines develop organically into larger units: presbytery, parish hall, bookshop and nursery-school can be grouped round the church as their centre. Such a parish centre, open in its turn to the surrounding world, can become the spiritual power-house of a modern suburb. There are fine examples of such units in Metzger's St. Francis at Riehen and Baur's St. Michael's at Hirzbrünnen (Bâle).

Any discussion of church-building today must include the problem of the repair or rebuilding of damaged or ruined churches. What is the right way to build in such cases? Should a church that has been destroyed be replaced by a copy of it? Should parts which

26

have been destroyed be restored in the style of the old, or in that of contemporary building? In our opinion, the earlier ages of European architectural style show the right procedure. In the case of minor repairs, they followed the old style. But considerable replacements, or new buildings on an old site, were done as a matter of course in contemporary style. How successful they were can be seen in the combination of Gothic choirs with Romanesque naves, and the pleasant harmony of Baroque naves with Gothic choirs.

The question can also arise whether it is possible to enlarge an old church when it has become too small for present needs. We should advise against such enlargement. It is very seldom successful. Generally speaking, the old church is ruined and the new, compromise structure proves inadequate in size in another few years. If an old church is too small, it is better to leave it intact and build a new one in addition to it.

PAINTING AND SCULPTURE IN CHURCH

A comparison of modern churches with those of the last of the great European styles, Baroque, confirms the conclusion reached in our survey of Christian and ecclesiastical art in the nineteenth and twentieth centuries: there is scarcely any place in contemporary churches for the traditional type of ecclesiastical sculpture. In a Baroque church it has its place, both as statuary and as bas-relief, on the high altar, the choir-benches, the pillars of the nave and in the side-chapels. In the modern church the altar has been restored to its archetypal form, the table; it has no use for altar-pieces and the opportunities they offer for painting and sculpture. And pillars, aisles and clustering side-chapels have all given way to the unity of an interior centred on the *one* altar.

But the conclusion that the Church has no further need of the creative artist would be a mistaken one. If we can rid ourselves of the narrow nineteenth-century concept of art, with its opposition between "art" in the sense of pictures and statues and the applied arts and crafts, and get back to the idea of the artist's task as the making of all the things needed in the House of God, from candlesticks to murals, we shall see how wide and rewarding a field the modern church offers in the fields both of painting and of sculpture, The new form it has taken requires them to take a new position and a new direction, but not to disappear.

The altar is still a high theme for art. Its shape is now that of the archetypal table, chest or slab. These are basic sculptural forms. In an altar, they achieve their artistic value not by applied ornamentation but out of the basic shapes and relationships of the surface and the lower structure. Since 1925, modern altars have shown a development corresponding to the course of modern architecture. The large, heavy blocks of the earlier period have become smaller, lighter and less solid. At Vence, Henri Matisse has made the

27

altar consist of a simple slab set on a round block, which is in fact a considerable fragment of a massive column. Its simple forms and bold, triangular outlines combine in a silhouette suggestive of a square tilted on one corner. The altar achieves a numinous equilibrium between mass and lightness which is characteristic of the architecture of the interior as a whole. A similar, more massive unity of altar, candles, cross and tabernacle can be seen in Bausenwein's altar in St. Kilian's in Schweinfurt. Both altars are completely simple in form; they are without ornament of any kind, but make full use of the colours and surface-qualities of their materials, both stone and metal. Albert Schilling, on the other hand, has clothed his altar-slab in the Church of All Saints at Bâle in a relief which combines symbol and colour in a higher unity. He has since successfully developed this kind of ornament, which does not obscure the character of the altar, in other Swiss churches, notably in the table-altar of the Church of Our Lady at Solothurn. Some beautiful, graceful altars have been produced by Hein Wimmer, Novarina (Audincourt) and H. and F. Maurer, whose altar at Berneck rests on the point of its three-cornered base. Gottfried Böhm has hit on a bold solution for St. Albert's at Saarbrücken: the base of the altar is a piece of modern, abstract sculpture, but the latter has no independent status of its own and exists solely as a contribution to the altar and the interior of the church as a whole. His altar in St. Columba's at Cologne is also, we consider, remarkably successful: a pyramid embedded half-deep in a cone resting on its own point, so that the base of the pyramid forms the altar-table. Base and top achieve unity together as a single stone of sacrifice.

Churches which are wholly concentrated upon one single altar naturally lead to a reawakening of the old desire to lay especial emphasis upon the altar. Builders and artists are once more taking an interest in altars with canopies and baldachinos. Hein Wimmer's design for the canopied altar in Our Lady's at Trier is successful and emphatic; Giefer and Mäckler (All Saints at Frankfurt) and Gottfried Böhm (St. Albert's at Saarbrücken) make it part of the architecture of the sanctuary. The baldachino has especially attracted the attention of Albert Schilling. In All Saints' at Bâle, the rectangular block of the altar is echoed by the plain rectangle of the baldachino, hung fairly low over the altar and repeating its themes with variations of colour and design. In St. Michael's at Hirzbrunnen (Bâle), Schiller uses a textile medium for the same idea. In St. Mary's at Olten he has combined the features of baldachino and canopy, surmounting the altar with a light span-roof.

For those artists who wish to serve the altar, the tabernacle offers a field of opportunities by no means limited to reliefs of symbolic or representational design in precious metals. We could wish that the painters would take as serious an interest in it as the sculptors have done (Wimmer, Bausenwein and Schilling have done outstanding work). It

28

seems to us that work in textiles, which has been so successfully developed in the case of vestments, would find an artistically rewarding and appropriate application in the tabernacle-veil.

The candlesticks, sanctuary lamp and liturgical vessels are subjects for plastic design which should be included in the plan of the church as a whole, and not left to chance and later occasions. The attempt to reduce them, in the early days of modern ecclesiastical art, to forms of the simplest functional significance, was not in any way a profanation but a necessary archetypal clarification (cf. the work of, e.g., Rudolf Schwarz, Fritz Schwerdt, Hein Wimmer, Elisabeth Treskow and Hildegard Domitzlaff). It is based upon history; earlier ages knew that the liturgical vessels were not originally symbols but functional objects, which only later acquired symbolic meaning. The way in which function can develop authenticity of form and artistic value can be seen, even in reproduction, in the candlesticks, chalices, monstrances, censers, croziers and rings produced by Schwarz, Wimmer, Schrage, Treskow, Jaeckel and Burch-Korrodi. They demonstrate that the artist can, in full confidence, embellish functional forms with symbolic figures and inscriptions: it is only necessary that these shall remain within the stylistic limits of the design of the object itself, and be subordinate to it. Here too we can discern a parallel development to that of architecture. There is an increase today in freedom and assurance, a confidence manifest in the monstrances and chalices of Mainrad Burch-Korrodi, which achieve an astonishing harmony of form with churches by Baur, Metzger and Schütz—a harmony which is certainly not a mere echo.

The development of liturgical vestments has followed a similar course. A return to simple forms meant an invitation to modern Christian expressive painting, with its massive forms and strong colours. It is deeply interesting that this kind of pictorial art has been as unsuccessful in vestments as on the altar. Several attempts have been made, of unquestionably high artistic value, and always the attention they concentrate upon themselves has meant a reduction of our sense of what is happening at the altar. Vestments which make massive or more attenuated use of liturgical colours, and of lettering and symbolic designs, seem to us more serviceable. The high unity of art and function attainable through these primary means can be seen in vestments by Matisse, Litzenburger, Erna Schilling and, especially, M. Augustina Flüeler.

When we turn from the altar to the body of the church, we at once come upon objects in the field of plastic art which seldom receive much attention and yet cry out for the artist's hand: altar-rails, pulpit and ambo, benches and confessional-boxes. If we look at them as they appear in churches by Schwarz, Baur and Metzger, or in the form given them by Hugo Kükelhaus in the College of St. Charles Borromeo at Münster and St. Boniface at

Dortmund, and then compare them with the common run of benches and rails, we can see the importance of their shape and arrangement from the liturgical point of view, and realise that even in such simple, unostentatious things a valid functional form can rise to the artistic level. There is nothing in the church which does not deserve the loving attention of an artist, whether it be a holy-water stoup, or casing for the organ, or furniture and fittings for the sacristy.

The font, an occasion of plastic art at its greatest during the Middle Ages, and later almost forgotten by artists, is once again being given a form worthy of the sacrament. There are fonts by Hein Wimmer, Hans Arp, and Albert Schilling in which functional and monumental qualities are combined with symbolism. The cover for the font—which is tending more and more towards the size of earlier days—affords obvious opportunities for plastic adornment; but as it is removed from the font and taken out of the baptistry at the time of a baptism, it makes no contribution to the performance of the ceremony. H. G. Bücher has hung the cover of his font in St. Boniface at Dortmund from the roof, so that when it is raised for a baptism the dove symbolising the Holy Ghost is left hovering over the water. He has put a candlestick beside the font which, outside Paschal time, holds the Paschal candle, from which the baptismal candle can be lit: thus the setting and the liturgy of baptism correspond to each other.

These works of art in the service of the church all make the fullest and most exacting demands on artist and patron alike; they represent a valid task, and at a high level, for the painter and sculptor. But this does not imply that there is no other place for art in the modern church. The altar must have a cross with the figure of Christ upon it. If we consider the crosses made by, e.g., Barlach, Marcks, Matisse, Wimmer, Bausenwein or Schwippert, whether directly intended for the altar or not, we can discern in them a common striving to make the crucifix a *sign*, strong, clear-cut and austere. The kingly Christ of the early Middle Ages and the Man of Sorrows, our brother, characteristic of our own time, seem to come together in one. The cross is sometimes placed upon the altar, sometimes suspended over it. In St. Kilian's in Schweinfurt, St. Canisius in Berlin and some churches in Switzerland, this has had the effect of combining the altar-cross with the triumphal cross.

The altar crucifix is the only image whose presence in the church the rubrics require. But it is customary for every church also to have an image of the Mother of God. So far as we can see, sculpture is more successful here than painting. The massive strength and austerity of Henry Moore's madonnas suggest the Mother of God and Queen of Heaven; Schürk-Frisch's madonna is a reminder that sculpture can also treat this lofty theme lightly and tenderly without thereby collapsing into sentimentality. Besides Christ crucified and the Mother of God, patrons and sculptors of an earlier day turned their attention to the

30

Man of Sorrows. Dinnendahl, Marcks and Mataré have approached this theme with a sure penetration which leaves no doubt of its special relevance to the image of God in men's minds today.

It is impossible not to see that many of these works of sculpture show traces of concealed historicism: reminiscences of early Romanesque or Irish art. We have already pointed out that this is the fate of most sculpture in our time. And it would be a mistake to point to the much-discussed crucifix and madonna at Assy, by Germaine Richter and Lipschitz respectively, as contrastingly modern and daring. For they are both doomed to the same concealed historicism, though of a different provenance. The crucifix belongs to late Impressionism, the madonna to impressionist Baroque.

Do these few themes and types exhaust the opportunities for painting and sculpture in church? Certainly not, but from there on they find their proper field not in the production of detachable works of art but once again as part of the architectonic structure of the church.

At first, the same types and techniques were applied to murals and glass in church as to ordinary pictures. Since the pioneer work done by Thorn-Prikker, they have taken the form of a multitude of individual images. Even the stained-glass windows at Assy, the masterpieces of Rouault, Manessier and Léger, are still determined by old types and techniques. The discovery of new forms and new techniques was made in the Sacré Coeur at Audincourt. Novarino gave his simple interior a strip of window running completely round it under the roof. Ferdinand Léger has made it the setting of a grand design in stained glass. The theme is the passion of Christ. It is not shown in direct portrayal of the events, but symbolised in emblems of the various stations and of the instruments of the passion. In his own characteristic way, which combines constructional forms with concrete emblems (Haftmann), Léger has succeeded in creating a great work. It is not in the old stained-glass technique, but built up of solid lumps of glass cemented together. It is technically part of the wall. The glowing, jewel-like colours and the emblems of the design belong together in a self-authenticating, convincing world of symbol. Léger has continued on his successful course in the windows of the extension of the church at Courfaivre in the Bernese Jura, which are again part of the architectonic structure. In contrast to the somewhat stiff, overdeliberate symbolism of the mosaics in the entrance hall at Assy, these windows have a certain serene inevitability.

The tendency of modern architecture to have whole walls in nothing but glass has given Georg Meistermann in St. Kilian's at Schweinfurt the chance of making the wall behind the altar a mere skeleton of cement, and filling it in with a symbolist design. In the Church of Our Lady at Solothurn, Schütz has given over the whole of the end wall to Hans

Stocker's stained glass. Both of these works, like Léger's windows, take their place as an integral part of the architecture of the church while heightening its effect.

In the church in Norderney and in various churches in Switzerland, Richard Seewald has prepared the ground for a new mural painting. What can be achieved in this field in the setting of modern architecture has been demonstrated by Matisse at Vence, with a very simple technique: the black drawings on the glossy walls and the non-representational designs of the windows combine to give the interior both distinction and a wonderful lightness and brightness. In St. Alphonsus at Würzburg, Hans Schädel and Georg Meistermann have achieved an astonishing degree of unity between the interior and the murals. It seems as though the whole church has been designed to set off the great murals of the Apocalypse, and as though the paintings, for their part, would be deprived of all meaning without their concentrated architectonic setting. Even the exterior of the church carries reminiscences of them. Other examples worth recording are the paintings flanking the entrance at Assy, by Léger, and at Audincourt, by Bazaine.

The genesis of these paintings is to be found in abstract and non-representational art. Yet anyone standing in any of these churches would hardly even be aware that he was looking at works of a controversial school. They combine representational forms, symbols, and masses of pure colour in a unity which raises no problems; the squabble over "meaningless" art here becomes meaningless. Plainly enough, attempts have been made to force painting of this sort into inappropriate subjects and settings; it cannot make a picture in itself, but achieves its purpose only within a greater architectural unity. On a small scale there is proof of this in Bazaine's baptistry at Audincourt, a non-representational composition in glass and concrete; a full-scale demonstration, in terms of the totality of a building, can be found in Marcel Breuer's plan for the monastery church at Collegeville, Minnesota: modern architecture, painting and sculpture unite in a totality which transcends them all to form the House of God for our times.

GOD'S TENT AMONG MEN

If we try to give ourselves a general account of the forms taken by modern churches, we may find ourselves being reminded of a remark made by Hans Schwippert at a conference in Darmstadt in 1951. "In this age," he said, "marked as it is by unrest, fear and foreboding, something is manifesting itself among architects all over the world as though it were a mighty law of building; something which has nothing to do with the constriction, trouble, unrest and fear of these days. Does it not seem remarkable that in the years in which devastation came upon us, in years when we do not know what further devastations may be before us, we should, all round the world, respond to a law of building which has

32

nothing to do with strongholds and refuges? That, all over the world, instead of building strong refuges, good architects are building tents, light, wide-open things? And does not this following out of the command within us cut strangely across the more obvious demands of human reason?"

Let us take Fritz Metzger's Church of SS. Felix and Regula in Zürich (1950) as an example. The plan consists of irregular curves and right-angles, avoiding the definite geometrical shapes of older buildings; it has flexibility. This flexible, open plan is matched by the open, articulated construction of walls and roof. The wall no longer carries the weight of the building. It is simply a light curtain enclosing the interior, and is surmounted by a strip of window. The supporting columns slant up to the roof like the poles of a tent, and the roof itself is a multiplicity of swelling, overlapping forms. This is the result, not of any deliberate attempt but of the plain, obvious way of constructing a simple, light interior concentrated upon the altar; and the effect is absolutely that of God's tent pitched amid the storms of time.

As in the case of secular buildings, God's tent among men today is the result of adapting the two types of hall developed by the industrial architecture of the nineteenth century: the rectangular workshop and the round-roofed exhibition-hall. Starting from these two basic types, new types have developed in ecclesiastical architecture; types which hardly seem to recall their point of departure, but which follow, in their several ways, the common tendency towards the tent-form. Are they a true response to this age and its people? Can they take their stand before the face of God? The liturgical section of this book will have made a closer consideration of the old idea of the Tent of God. The church as God's Tent is certainly a legitimate Christian concept. Whether it also corresponds in a deeper sense to this age and its people, whether it may perhaps be *the* right form for the church to take in our times, will be discussed in later sections: "From the Basilica to the Tent of God," and "The Position of Modern Art in History."

THE PATRON'S RESPONSIBILITY

To have a successful church, we must assume that we have a gifted architect; and, where furnishings and images are concerned, a serious artist. But no less necessary is the understanding, or at the very least the good will, of the patron. In our judgments of modern architecture, we are often too apt to forget the decisive and responsible part played by the patron and contracting authority in determining what sort of new building shall eventually result. A church, like any other building, should be the result of co-operation between architect and patron. Architects today do not have any complaints to make about the general readiness of patrons to take part in the work. But they do consider that it is the wrong part.

People are very ready to plunge into questions of architecture and style, demanding alterations here and finding fault there until the original plan is completely ruined. But the architect's enquiries about general and local liturgical requirements are often left unanswered. Other artists make the same complaint. What they want are definite iconographical specifications and precise information about the kind of picture or statue wanted and the setting in which it is to be placed; what they get are criticisms of modern style. Now these questions put by architects and artists are the key to the patron's own sphere in the building of the church. What a joy it should be for him to throw open the whole world of iconography, with all its rich possibilities, to an artist; or to inspire an architect to bear in mind the liturgy of the consecration of a church when he is drawing plans for the house of God. What a splendid task he will be setting himself if he looks beyond the completion of the church to the building of a "parochial unit," with nursery school, school, house of hospitality, bookshop and presbytery all clustering organically round the church; and if he extends his plans to include the cemetery and the problem of its headstones.

Good architects have long since worked out plans for such "parochial units"; and sculptors have long since achieved grave-stones of worth and dignity. It has always been the privilege of the patron to give his architect and artists directions concerning the requirements of the cult and of local conditions. But we should do well to remember that when it came to purely artistic and stylistic questions, the great patrons of Europe's past have not considered themselves authorities.

The patron should realise that the building of the church begins with himself and his parish. It is part of his task to arrange that the architect and the other artists shall be working together from the planning stage. This is the only way to make the church artistically successful as a whole. We complain because so few architects and artists undertake work for the Church. If we ask great architects, painters or sculptors the reason for their avoidance of it, they reply that they have never received commissions for such work. Younger artists give the same answer. We must not forget that the patron has to be the starting-point in ecclesiastical art. He ought not to entrust his work solely to the old hands in the business of "religious art," whom he finds coming to him very much like commercial travellers; nor even simply go off to a reliable dealer for his vessels and vestments. Instead, he should look out for real artists, give them a chance, leave them sufficient time, and await results with patience. If he has no personal knowledge of an architect or artist to whom he can entrust the fulfilment of his ideas with a clear conscience, he should go, with confidence, to someone who does understand contemporary art. There is nothing irresponsible in this.

Interference in strictly artistic matters is often done in the name of the feelings of the parish. Anyone with any experience of "opinion research" will agree that it is extremely

34

difficult—or rather, impossible—to give an accurate representation of the opinion of a community. It is also worth remembering that history affords no examples of works of art produced by majority vote. Anyone who really thinks about the Christian parish and its present situation will be more likely to decide in favour of modern church architecture, art and design. We are told today that our European countries are turning from Christian countries into missionary territories. One of the Church's basic maxims, in the missions, is not only to talk the language of the people but to build churches in their style of architecture. Those who desire to be missionaries to Europe's masses ought, according to this, to build churches which correspond to their kind of building: which means churches in modern architecture.

The ecclesiastical patron can do today what he has always done: give legitimate contemporary art its chance. The historical situation at this time, as we have tried to sketch it, should be borne in mind. It is a time of beginnings, and like all beginnings it needs simplicity and discipline. But the patron or artist who accepts its limitations will be serving not only his own time but the future as well. It is hard, indeed, for a human being still in the grip of an illusion of happiness, and for an artist with one foot still in the age of individual fame, to accept the idea of living in a primitive age and making of his life and his work a sacrifice to be built into the foundations of a new epoch. But life and work in such an age are not without historic significance; the preliminary clearing of the ground and digging of foundations may be no less important in the erection of a new thousand-year palace of art, than the final ceremony of crowning it with its panoply of towers.

THE INSTRUCTIO DE ARTE SACRA

What has the Church to say in the discussion of these problems? The attitude of the Catholic Church is summarised, in its main lines, in the *Instructio de arte sacra* issued on the 30th June 1952 by the Supreme Congregation of the Holy Office. This Instruction has been the subject of numerous misunderstandings and wild generalisations. Some attribute to an Instruction the nature, to all intents and purposes, of a dogma; others read meanings into it of which there is no mention in the text.

The Instruction gives general directions on the building of churches, their interior architecture, and their furnishing with pictures, statues, and liturgical objects. The church is to be conceived as the House of God and of prayer. It is to be simple and practical, without false ornamentation, but plainly different from a secular building. The interior must conform to liturgical law. It should "sustain the faith and piety of those who come into the church to assist at divine worship and to beg for heavenly gifts." Individual works of art within it should also be designed to assist the liturgy and the worship of the congregation.

35

They must not be offensive to religious feeling or unworthy of the holy place. The church is not the place for experiment any more than for mass-produced figures of the usual trashy sort. Finally, standards in church art shall be set by Christians who are not only experts in their own fields but are living and working on the basis of the faith.

The Instruction has been accused of being hostile to contemporary art in its present form, and forbidding it to Christians. There is no question of this either in the text of the Instruction or in the commentary provided by the *Osservatore Romano*. The Instruction is not so sensational as it might seem. In fact it simply brings together a number of provisions already existing in Canon Law and particular decrees, and enjoins a stricter observance of them. Their purpose is limited to indicating the scope and limitations of art in the service of the Church. They do not embark on questions of style and form, and certainly do not provide guidance in aesthetics, still less detailed recipes for Christian artists; which means that they are much more moderate than the instructions often given in Germany, for instance, to architects by those commissioning them.

It gives us no grounds to fear a fixation of church art at a particular stage of its development, nor its isolation from the living stream of creative art. It cites laws of the Councils of Nicaea and of Trent, and other regulations of many centuries' standing. A glance at the history of Western art is enough to show that they have not hindered the development of church art as a living thing embodying the forms of its own age. The greatest misunderstanding has been directed to the prohibition on erecting unusual statues. This has been applied to modern art-forms, but this is out of the question. We have already seen that church art is primarily a matter of iconography. Hence, unusual images should be interpreted as meaning not works in a modern style but, in accordance with the long-standing law of the Church, innovations in iconography. Photographically naturalist painters and owners of "church art factories" have no cause for rejoicing. In his commentary, Cardinal Celso Costantini, the Holy See's authority on Christian art and the organiser of the great Holy Year exhibitions in 1950, has given an explicit warning to bishops and pastors not to place unthinking reliance on such people. He stresses the truth that the great masters have always been the supreme representatives of their own time. He knows that the art of our time is a matter of clearing ground and of new departures. It is by no means to be excluded from the church. But the Church expects an artist who wishes to make things for her to "submit himself to the spirit of tradition in art and the liturgy." Art's new impulses must be wedded to the timeless truths of the faith.

Thus what Pope Pius XII says in his encyclical *Mediator Dei* (1947) is of fundamental importance: "Modern pictures and statues, whose style is more adapted to the materials in use at the present day, are not to be condemned out of hand. On condition that these modern

36

arts steer a middle course between an excessive realism on the one hand and an exaggerated symbolism on the other, and take into account more the needs of the Christian community than the personal taste and judgment of the artist, they should be allowed full scope if with due reverence and honour they put themselves at the service of our churches and sacred rites."

However, the Instruction does set itself against certain particular manifestations of contemporary art. It allows no place in the church to experiment. Obviously, this is not a total rejection. Costantini ascribes a healthy and purifying effect to experiment. But it does not belong inside a church. We should not overlook the fact that the Instruction is exclusively concerned with *church* art. The creation and exhibition of Christian works of art outside the walls of the church are matters left to the mentality and responsibility of the individual.

This attitude on the part of the Church is not new. It is part of the custom of the centuries. The church is primarily a place for the cult; it exists for the sake of the sacrifice offered by the community. It is not to be wondered at that the Church has continued, since the Middle Ages, to insist that works of art in church shall be subject to the laws of an imagery above the subjective, personal level so as to make its appeal to all alike. But this does not mean that she rejects new forms of Christian imagery. The devotional images which began to appear in the fourteenth century, for instance, were not suppressed, but they were not admitted inside the church. Tenderly devotional presentations of the Mother of Sorrows or Christ and St. John would have their place in convent cells or chapels, where they would assist private devotion. When, at a later date, they did find their way into the churches, they were allotted side-chapels, which again are places of silent individual prayer. In the same way today, a greater latitude of choices of images than is suitable to a parish church would be allowable for monastic chapels or other places of worship serving a definite, limited community, such as universities, schools and prisons.

There is no question in the Instruction of imposing a featureless uniformity. It has no intention of turning local Roman style into something compulsory for the whole Church. That is not the way of the Roman Curia in such questions. For what can answer our needs as a Christian image, whether in church or in our own homes, can perfectly well vary, though without any fundamental disharmony, from one part of the world and from one individual country to another.

FROM THE BASILICA TO THE TENT OF GOD

We need some historical basis for saying that the modern church, as God's tent, corresponds to our age and its religion in the same way as did the churches of Europe's past history. We must try to get further back into the history of art, and view Western art as a whole. We must try to achieve a vantage point from which we can see the decades and centuries forming into periods, and, in each period, just those works which contributed to the creation of its style, the kind of men who gave the age its leaders, and the idea that it had of God.

What was the situation when the West was beginning, about A.D. 330? The Christian church is the basilica. Does it correspond to the leading group among men? The leaders in 330 are still the soldiers and officials of Rome, with the Emperor at their head. The basilica-church certainly corresponds to them. It is an extension and development of the assembly-room and the hall of justice and commerce of the later Empire, presided over by the statue of the divine Emperor. If we look at the pictures of Christ and the Apostles in the mosaics of Christian basilicas, we shall see that they are reminiscent, in spirit and attitude, of the statues of the Emperors and their officials. The Christians saw Christ as the successor of the Emperor, as the Divine Imperator.

Roman basilicas were still being built in Europe about the year 800. But they are easy to recognise as leftovers, imitations, no longer really of their own time. The more character-istic architectural form is the fortress-like tower now being built at the west end of the basilica, with an entrance-hall at the bottom and a chapel on the second and third floors (as at Corvey). It was a combination of the round temple of antiquity and the stone-course building of the north, cave and tower in one, this first style produced by the West. Alois Fuchs has identified its status as being that of royal chapel.[1] Does this too correspond to the ruling caste of the period and its idea of God? It might well be so; it was a time when Germanic warriors were turning into a landed warrior-nobility, with the king as army-leader at their head. Considered as an order of society, its centre is the fortress-tower of the royal palace. We know from literary sources that these men thought of Christ as the King's Son. Ninth- and tenth-century images of Him confirm it. They present Him as crucified, but not as the Man of Sorrows: this is a Christ without wounds or suffering, a strong, dark symbol of royalty upon the Cross.

By about 1200, these landed warriors have become knights; the desire for Christian virtue and culture is having a determining effect upon life, and the high ideal of leadership is embodied in the Emperor. The centre of ordinary life is the castle, huge and beautiful, dominating the landscape. There are knights who dedicate their whole lives to the Lord in monasteries which, in turn, are like castles. Out of the Roman basilica and the fortress-tower come the rich and splendid cathedrals of Germany and France: one in spirit, despite the distinction between "Romanesque" and "Gothic"—Castles of God, as the chroniclers call them. Here Christ reigns as a high and noble Lord, inclining, in a heavenly type of

[1] "Entstehung und Zweckbestimmung der Westwerke," *Westfälische Zeitschrift*, Vol. 100, Münster, 1952.

chivalrous love, towards Mary; loyal and generous, the knight follows in His train, as in this world he follows the Emperor on his progress through the Empire.

By about 1450 the world has changed. It is the age of the bourgeois, humanist and cultivated—or at any rate paying homage to the ideal of humanism. The greatest moments of his day are those spent in some Renaissance palace, conversing with men like-minded with himself and feasting his eyes on scholars and discoverers, statesmen and condottieri. The church becomes, exteriorly, a magnificent palace; interiorly, a hall where the humanist can meet Christ the Hero in company with the saints. The latter appear on the great altar-pieces on the same level as Christ, conversing with Him—a Christ with the beautiful, unveiled body of a hero of antiquity. Churches of this period north of the Alps are in the same spirit, even if they do still have the spires of Gothic cathedrals. Inside, they are halls of the bourgeois city, a whole age and a changed world away from the last of the cathedrals, those thirteenth-century Castles of God, with their sense of danger without and mystical fire within.

By about 1700 the West is drawing to its close. A polite, hierarchical society sets the tone, in which the humanist, enlightened bourgeoisie and nobility can meet and mingle. Its culminating image is that of the absolutist prince, and the background to its spacious living is the Baroque castle, set in its formal landscape. Its great state-room, where the prince receives his people, answers to the interiors of the churches of the period, which often stand with a monastery, built, like the castles, into the landscape. In such a church, ceremonious and exuberant in form and colour, Christ as the Heavenly Sovereign awaits the homage of His subjects. The church becomes "God's salon."

We give here a table intended to summarise this succession of the different groups taking the lead in society, and their churches and images of Christ, during the various periods of Western art from the fourth to the eighteenth century. For completeness, we have added a corresponding summary of our own time. We shall shortly go on to a fuller discussion of the relationship between society, the church, and its imagery in the twentieth century.

This brief historical sketch is not intended as a contribution to the potted simplifications served up, under pain of damnation by Jacob Burckhardt, to an age which prefers such treatment. We know very well that history was a great deal more manifold and complex than may appear from our survey. But an adequate discussion of the different periods and the creative forces at work in them is not the subject of this book. Yet even sketches can have their meaning, restoring clarity and emphasis to certain basic features which we are apt to lose sight of in studying more detailed problems and periods. We consider that these basic features suffice to answer the historical questions raised by this book.

Our survey of the history of art in the West has shown that in every period church archi-

39

Ruling group	Its characteristic building	Idea of God	Type of church	Type of image
C. 400: Soldiers and officials of the later Empire, culminating in the Emperor	Hall of justice and commerce (basilica)	Christ as Emperor	Basilica	Christ in the guise of a Roman Emperor
C. 800: Germanic warriors turning into a landed nobility, culminating in the King as army-leader	Royal palace and fortified tower	Christ as the King's Son	The royal chapel in the West Tower	Christ the King on the Cross
C. 1200: The Christian knight and knightly monk, culminating in the Emperor	Castle	Christ as the mild and noble Lord of heaven and earth	The cathedral—Castle of God	Christ as the fair and knightly Lord of heaven and earth
C. 1450: Humanist bourgeois, culminating in the scholar, statesman and condottieri of the renaissance	Renaissance palace	Christ as the humanist Hero of heaven	The palace and great hall of God	Christ as the Hero, conversing with Apostles and Saints
C. 1700: Hierarchical court-society, culminating in the apotheosis of the absolutist prince	Baroque castle	Christ as the heavenly Sovereign	Christ's hall of state in God's castle	Christ triumphant in the hierarchy of heaven
C. 1950: Technical industrial workers, homeless and looking for "redemption"	Tent-like steel-frame construction, originating in industrial buildings: "The tent of Labour"	Christ the Redeemer	The Tent of God	Christ our Brother and Redeemer

tecture has represented a sublimation of the building characteristic of the ruling class of the period. The great cathedrals of the twelfth and thirteenth centuries do not continue to be dour, fortress-like royal towers but reveal themselves as Castles of God, on the same ample scale as the contemporary castles of the Emperor and the knights, and so setting the sacral crown upon that golden age of the West. The city church of the Renaissance is in no way reminiscent of a Gothic castle but of the palaces of those men who set the tone of the age; and the Baroque period—despite undertones of apparent historicism—not only built new churches in its own style but was very ready to cover the interiors of old ones with its own lavish decorations.

The relationship of ecclesiastical art to tradition was never a matter of rejecting contemporary style in favour of historicism. The Church's great architectural achievements from the West Tower at Corvey to the French cathedrals and on to St. Peter's and Balthasar Neumann's Vierzehnheiligen pilgrims' church have all been supremely of their own time.

Let us leave European history now, and look for the leading class of our own day and the building characteristic of it. The leadership belongs without doubt to the man without a home, the man who works in industry and technics and the management of them. The building characteristic of him is an industrial building. The fact that other buildings in this age have taken the architectural forms developed in industry and adapted them to their own needs is simply an application of this ancient law of art which remains valid in every period. When architects set about using this style—now tending towards the tent-form—for the benefit of church-building, they are conforming to the same law. They are sublimating the secular architecture characteristic of the age to make a church adequate to its needs— as European architects have always done before. We may, then, complete our schematic survey somewhat as follows, bringing it down to 1950:

Leading class: Homeless technical and industrial workers. Characteristic building: "Tent of Labour," tent-like steel-frame structure, deriving its forms from industrial architecture. Church: the Tent of God.

The question of the corresponding idea and image of God remains an open one. In the opinion of Müller-Erb, the working man of our time sees Christ as his Brother. Supposing we enquire of contemporary art. The pictures and statues of the last few decades, especially the crucifixes and statues of the Man of Sorrows, show us Christ as the Redeemer, reminding the ravaged and broken men of this catastrophic century of His sacrifice, admonishing them as brothers, and taking them to Himself. There can be no doubt that Christ the Redeemer stands in the foreground of our concept of God today. The cry for redemption is the cry of the masses, even though it may be articulated in un-Christian or even atheistic formulae.

So our scheme can be completed by adding: Idea of God: Redeemer. Image: Christ as Brother and Redeemer.

These additions to our scheme are, of course, made with all the tentative reserve necessary when writing contemporary history. But it is perfectly obvious that this image of Christ as the brotherly Redeemer on the one hand, and the interiors of modern churches on the other, correspond to each other in an amazing way. If we look at the position of the altar in the churches of the last few decades, it is plain that ever since the Perret brothers' churches and Moser's Church of St. Antony, there has been a steady change in one direction: the congregation has been coming nearer and nearer to the altar. In the churches of our time, He stands fraternally—though in a seemly detachment—in the midst of the people gathered for the sacrifice. Another point worthy of some thought, and one which again lends support to our scheme, is that these churches also represent at its highest level the sociological tendency in modern architecture: their rejection of the enclosed units of an earlier style of building, their use of open plan, their free, wide-open interiors are a manifestation of the striving to lead man out of his isolation in an exaggerated individualism into brotherly intercourse with his fellowman, and so into true community.

Our excursion into the history of art has confirmed our view that churches in modern architecture represent the legitimate form of the church for our time, and the pictures, statues and furnishings corresponding to it the legitimate form of church art.

Are there other facts in the history of art which could be advanced to destroy the historical basis for this thesis? Our view that the Christian church in the West has always been, as a building, supremely contemporary might be contradicted by citing Late Gothic, which ran parallel, in the North, to the Italian Renaissance, and even sent active offshoots down into the age of Baroque. The problems of the relation between Late Gothic and Renaissance architecture, and Late Gothic, Jesuit-Gothic and Baroque have not yet been satisfactorily studied from an artistic point of view. But what is certain is that this northern Late Gothic cannot be compared with the Gothic of the cathedrals. The most that can be said for it is to regard its interiors, especially in the case of the hall type of church, as the northern equivalent of the *aula* of the Italian Renaissance. Its more wild and extravagant offshoots, and "Jesuit-Gothic" as well, may be regarded as northern varieties of Baroque.

We have seen that past ages always built their churches in the style of their own time. Our historical survey of the nineteenth century pointed out that its new forms of art never involved any radical break with the past. On the contrary, they developed organically out of the forms which preceded them, according to laws valid at any period. When we come to discuss the historical standpoint of our own time, we shall see even more clearly how closely linked with tradition our modern architects and artists are in their creative work.

42

The accusation is made that modern churches are not "religious." Is it seriously thought that imitating the style of a past age makes a church religious? It seems to us that this notion of the meaning of "religious" comes near to being sentimental rubbish.

A church always succeeds in being religious, i.e. validly itself, when an architect with artistic talent has applied himself to meeting the requirements of the liturgy with the means which his own contemporary style places at his disposal. A truly religious interior has never been the fruit of deliberate historicism; it comes into existence as a genuine statement of reality, as at this present moment, in architectural terms. And it is entirely beside the point for those who stand for an historically conservative style in Christian churches to cite Chinese and Egyptian temples in their support.

Modern architecture is criticised for its new-fangled materials, and demands are made that only "well-tried building methods and thoroughly down-to-earth materials" be used. Iron, concrete and glass are as down-to-earth as any material can be; they would pass muster even by magical standards, coming as they do out of the earth itself. Methods of building and materials have always, at every period, been determined by the technical and financial resources of the time. Art did not deteriorate, still less come to an end, when the Stone Age gave way to the Bronze Age. Gothic architecture did not become un-Christian and worthless in Lower Germany because it there made use of plain brickwork, though to the architects of France and the Rhineland, and travellers from the West generally, this meant something new. Northern churches of the Baroque period did not become insignificant and trashy because they made magnificent use of the new material of stucco as a substitute for marble in pillars and cornices. Glass, iron and concrete are the materials which correspond to our needs. As with the materials of every other age, they can be made into either good or bad architecture.

The objection is brought against the Tent of God that it is not an idea of our time, but an old one. The idea of the Castle of God is just as old. Yet its architectural realisation did not come in the days of early Christianity, but in the high Middle Ages. We have seen why. It need be no more a matter of chance or arbitrary choice that the old idea of the Tent of God is making its way into architecture today. A glance at our century is enough to indicate why its hour should have struck now. Surrounded by catastrophes which are also technical achievements, and living in an age of migrations, the man of this century has realised that there is no building so strong that it can offer him the security of a safe refuge. Perhaps we are seeing ourselves nowadays as the people of God on its wanderings in the wilderness, impermanent and precarious; perhaps we are beginning to translate the portable Tabernacle of that time into a church which is the Tent of God, light and quick to set up again after each fresh catastrophe.

43

THE POSITION OF MODERN ART IN HISTORY

We are still faced with the fact of active historicism at work in the kind of art of which we are speaking, and it is fair to ask how we should interpret the juxtaposition of these Romanesque and Gothic reminiscences with the modern Tent of God: is it something arbitrary, or a manifestation of "historical logic"? We will make the question the occasion of an attempt to establish where we stand today in the history of art, and what kind of an age this may prove to be.

We have said that in the great periods of European art, historicism in the nineteenth- and twentieth-century sense was unknown. We must make a correction. The statement applies only to the Middle Ages and after. In the early ages of the West, from about 400 to 1000, we constantly encounter a similar historicism in architecture and art. The West Tower of the Carolingian age, which we took as our first type of Western architecture, stands beside buildings which rear their marble columns, golden roofs and fifth-century-style Roman mosaics against the northern sky. The Carolingian renaissance was a vast, state-organised piece of historicism, a last attempt (on such a scale) to bring the forms of late Roman Imperial art to life again. It failed, because history had already taken its own legitimate steps to preserve the heritage of Rome.

The centuries from about A.D. 400 to 800 present violent contrasts in the field of art. Confronting the Roman basilicas, we have the cave-like stone-courses of the Irish churches. Alongside Roman statues and paintings, with their naturalistic plastic presentation of man, appears the non-representational, "abstract" art of the Germanic peoples, Europe's new lords. Both styles survive, in uncompromising contrast, beyond the age of Charlemagne; both finally die of historicism. Europe's new art develops from a synthesis of the Roman and Germanic forms, and in response to demands made by Christians upon architecture and the visual arts. This long and complicated process had begun even before Charlemagne. Research into the period is still incomplete; few works of art remain from that time; they do not suffice for a reconstruction of the whole process. But we can see the slow regression in the highly developed visual forms of Roman art. They become simpler, more abstract, and so come to approximate more closely to the forms of Germanic art, which for their part are not fully comprehensible in terms of the modern idea of "ornament." It seems that Germanic art also underwent a simplification, which eventually made it possible for the two to meet at a sort of rock-bottom-level of form, at once an end and a beginning.

Works showing this mutual penetration are to be found in Ireland: the bronze crucifixion in the Dublin Museum, and the paintings in early manuscripts of the Emerald Isle. Here we have the initial letters of biblical and liturgical texts made into glorious patterns of

44

shape and colour. They are at their best when they do not include figures and are entirely dependent on line and colour: "abstract art," the first genuine creation of Western painting, for such illumination was unknown to the Romans, and, obviously, to the early Germanic peoples. It is these initials which are the true legacy of the age in the field of painting, and not those pretty pictures, following historistically in the footsteps of antiquity, which we used to admire in manuscripts of the Carolingian renaissance. Here and there in the illuminations we find a suggestion of the human form: a head, which stands for the whole man. Even in the Dublin crucifixion the body of Christ is only suggested. The head and hands are there. The head is reduced to the simplest form, its expression wholly interiorised, full of a deep, primitive patience. Christ has no body, only a robe which is simply an outline to be filled in with the non-representational art of northern Germanic ornament. It is not an accident that this robe is also the stem of the cross itself, nor that the arms of Christ and of the cross unite to form the trumpet-shapes of Irish ornament.

This is the same early stage of synthesis as we saw before in the Carolingian West Tower; both stand amidst offshoots of historicism, equally individualist and full of presage for the future.

In those dark and troubled centuries, when visual form was appearing in such confused and contrasting shapes, Roman art was not being destroyed. Rather, it was being, so to say, melted down, so as to go on, changed but still living and active, into the new art now being created.

It seems to us that there are certain similarities between that early age in the West and the period since 1800. This is not to say that that age is now to be repeated, and that we ought to be building basilicas and copying Germanic ornament. Historical periods work in a different way from that: but we believe that their fundamental potentialities and tendencies do repeat themselves according to a certain rhythm. The course of art through time is spiral, constantly returning to an earlier point but at a different level and in a different way. Even in prehistoric art, we can discern a certain rhythmic alternation between more naturalistic and more symbolist and abstract periods.[1]

As the centuries after A.D. 400 saw a regression in Roman art, so we can see visual form in the West, since 1800, first running itself to death and then being deliberately dismantled. From Impressionism onwards, the development of painting may be seen as the progress of this work of reduction. Impressionism reduced natural form and the use of substantially true colour to shimmering surface-colour alone; the "Jugendstil" began to use things, hitherto expressed three-dimensionally, as flat decorative ornaments; Expressionism turned them into violently abstract primitive signs, pushed abstraction to its final conclusion where

[1] Adama van Scheltema, *Die Kunst der Vorzeit*, Stuttgart, 1950.

colour was concerned, and began to cultivate the wild and naïve, the "barbaric"—not now to be found in the north, but in Africa and the South Seas. Cubism split things up into their different visual surfaces, saw them simply as colour, and presented them as temporally serial experiences. Finally, the beginnings of abstract painting show Western form completely reduced to its elements. In the non-representational shapes and pure colours of one of Kandinsky's or Mondrian's geometrical compositions, we are perhaps down to rock bottom again. It may be once more both an end and a beginning.

This point—historically, a necessary and fruitful point—was reached in architecture in those first firmly anti-historicist buildings which, coldly practical, would admit only simple right-angles and the undisguised, unsoftened materials of the technical age: early buildings from the Bauhaus circle and the Dutch *stijl* group, and Le Corbusier's "machines for living in."

Does this mean the final stage in the "decline of the West"? By no means; anyone who follows the course of painting and sculpture from Delacroix down to our own day will get the impression that these works are extraordinarily closely related to the great styles of Europe's past. It seems almost as though our best painters and sculptors have been, unintentionally, recapitulating the whole development of Western art, but backwards and at great speed. Baroque is latent in the Impressionists, especially Renoir. It is there in Rodin's sculpture too, as Joseph Ganther has shown in his book on Rodin and Michelangelo (Vienna, 1953). Cézanne's pictures were at first in the same spirit (e.g. "La douleur" in the Louvre); but his landscapes soon assume the austerity of a latent Renaissance style. Gothic is at work in German Expressionism, among the "Brücke" painters and in Barlach's sculpture; and there is an undercurrent of Romanesque in Rouault's glass and Marck's statues. Modern architecture, and especially church architecture, has followed a similar course.

Here we have the parallel to the early ages of the West. Then, by a long, painful artistic process the heritage of Rome was melted down and passed on, changed but still living, to the new age; today, it seems, the same thing is being done for the West itself. What is happening in modern art is not the end of the West but the historical preservation of its spirit. It is modern architects and artists who stand firm in tradition; they are tools of history. The historicists, on the other hand, can no longer do anything for the thing which they believe they are defending against the "innovators"; they have fled into one of history's blind alleys.

NEW POSSIBILITIES

Our historical comparison is not to be taken literally. History does not literally repeat itself. No doubt everything will happen again, perhaps everything has happened already,

46

but on a different level, in a different way and with different values. So it would be historically unsound to bring against the position we have taken the objection that our recapitulation idea may have indicated *one* of the roots of modern art, and also provided grounds for a comparison with the early ages of the West, but that we have not given our modern parallels to Christianity and the Germanic peoples, as the two great forces in that earlier age. But who knows how many forces may be going to work together in the age to come? Still, there is certainly one force in our present time which may be compared with the Germanic peoples in the early days of Europe: science and the techniques built upon it, with their abstract forms and formulae, certainly one of the present forces in history.

Since the close of the great age of the West, science has changed Europe and the world and our whole existence in a way which certainly bears comparison with the changes beginning with the Germanic invasions of the Roman Empire. Its effect on art is, in the case of architecture, obvious. But neither painting nor sculpture can escape it either. What the final outcome of this encounter will be, no one can say. There is food for thought in Romano Guardini's comment on this situation, in *Das Ende der Neuzeit* (Würzburg, 1951)[1]: "Nature (in the sense operating in science and technics) has withdrawn to a distance, so that direct relationship with it is no longer possible. It can no longer be conceived visually but only abstractly. It has become more and more a complex arrangement of relations and functions, expressible only in mathematical symbols and dependent on something to which no definite name can now be given. This new nature can no longer be felt—or at any rate only with feelings of a very fine-spun, marginal nature: as the utterly alien, ineffable, inaccessible. But we must be wary even here. For this, too, probably involves new tasks and opportunities. It may be that the limits of experience are being extended, so that things will come to belong to the world of experience which could not hitherto be felt. But it may be, too, that a kind of indirect extra sense is being developed, by which things which had their place hitherto only in abstract thinking will become part of actual living. Perhaps this development may link up with abstract art."

Jean Gebser, in his *Ursprung und Gegenwart* (Stuttgart, 1949 and 1953), has some consoling ideas about this pushing back of the frontiers which, incidentally, bear out our thesis concerning the survival of the West, in a changed form, within the new age. He believes that the age of perspective is to be followed by the age of aperspective, and that man will achieve an integral level of consciousness and arrive at a conscious totality which will embrace both the past and the future as present. The formal products of the spirit of such an age will be in the medium of transparency.

[1] English translation *The End of the Modern World* (New York, Sheed & Ward, 1956).

47

We have already seen that this opinion is confirmed by modern architecture. The tents it produces delight in great transparent sheets of glass; other walls, again, dissolve in a multiplicity of openings; interiors become light, airy, transparent and unobstructed. And finally, it is possible for these new forms to let the basic features of past styles as it were shine through them.

If we look at our age as the beginning of a new epoch, recognise science and technics as forces in history, and interpret the art of our time in accordance with this situation, we find ourselves confronted with opposition from Christians in particular. They think all this means proclaiming the end of Christianity. It appears that their support for historicist Christian art is a result of this opinion. It is true, indeed, that *other* religions have come to an end with the end of an age and its art. They collapsed with the nations and empires to which they belonged. But unlike these ancient religions, Christianity today is limited to no single people, no particular group, no part of the world. Friedrich Heer has given his opinion, in *Das Experiment Europa* (Einsiedeln, 1952), that this world-wide Church, having outgrown the constrictions and limitations of old Europe, is going to usher in the first fully authentic age of Christianity. If he is right, then this gives us the character of the religious component in the art of the future. It is at least worth some thought that modern architecture and art, like the Church, are not limited to any one part of the world, but have gained a foothold wherever Christianity has established itself. For a religion to be spread over every part of the world is something new and unique in religious history; for a style to be accepted all over the world is something equally unprecedented in the history of art.

THEODOR FILTHAUT

Church Art and the Liturgy

THE LORD'S HOUSE

It is no mysterious theological speculation, but simply the witness of Holy Scripture which calls Christians the "house of God" (1 Tim. 3, 15) and the "habitation of God" (Eph. 2, 22). Unlike the pagans, who worshipped the divinity in the form of a divine image set up in a temple, the faithful knew that "God dwelleth not in temples made with hands" (Acts 17, 24). As Christ Himself called His physical body a temple (John 2, 19 ff.), so His mystical body, the Church, is the Temple of God. It is not mere rhetoric when St. Paul declares that "You are the temple of the living God" (2 Cor. 6, 16). The faithful *are* that temple, because they have become in a special sense the property of their Lord. They are the Ecclesia, i.e., the assembly of those who have been called out of this world by God through His Word—Jesus Christ—and given His grace. This means that they may also truly be called the Church—*Kyriake*—i.e., those who belong to the Lord. "But Christ is as the Son in his own house: which house are we, if we hold fast the confidence and glory of hope unto the end" (Heb. 3, 6). We shall miss the concrete significance of this image if we fail to realise that it refers to the real presence of God in the believer. Over and above His omnipresence, God is present in man through faith in a new mode which transcends everything in nature. Christ says of this indwelling: "We will come to him and will make our abode with him" (John 14, 23). So we shall completely misunderstand this "house of the living God" if we regard it as a "purely" spiritual temple. The people of God is a "spiritual house" (1 Peter 2, 5), which here means something essentially different from a thing of pure spirit. It is because they are built up in the Holy Spirit that the Apostle calls the faithful a "spiritual house." This has nothing to do with the distinction within nature between spirit and matter; it refers to the new kind of existence conferred by Christ in the Spirit of God. This existence involves the whole man, spirit and body alike. Hence the people of God is a visible society. Hence St. Paul can say: "Know you not that your members are the temple of the Holy Ghost, who

49

is in you?" (1 Cor. 6, 19). Being a society of bodily creatures, the people of God receives its new spiritual life in the form of a mystery, i.e., under the veil of word and sign. And it needs an earthly environment in which to hear this word, to receive the gifts of the eternal kingdom, and to offer thanks and praise and petition: it needs that House of God which is built with stones. This exists for the sake of the community, or rather for the sake of the Lord, who comes here to meet His community in the celebration of the liturgy. This is the ground of the inconceivable dignity and holiness which attaches to a church. The ceremony of the dedication of a church sets this seal upon it as a holy place. This building is withdrawn from profane uses, set apart from the world, and made into the place where the People of God will celebrate its liturgy. But what is the liturgy? The liturgy of the Church is not, in its essence, simply a collection of beautiful, rich, interesting religious customs acquired and appropriated by the Church in the course of her long journey down the centuries. Even to understand it as "divine service" misses its essential character, if we take this to mean the service of man's praise, thanks, contrition, petition and offering. The determining factor in the Church's liturgy is the Incarnation of God in Jesus Christ. This does not simply mean that the liturgy celebrates the memory of the historical events of our Lord's life and work. It is that the liturgy is nothing less than the making present of Christ's redeeming work under the forms of a cult. Thus the Eucharist, for example, is the "memorial of the Lord" not only in the sense that there is a conscious recalling, in the minds of the congregation, of the life and works of their Kyrios, but in the precise and literal sense that the sacrifice of that Lord is here made really present. Is it necessary, in order to avoid misunderstanding, to point out that obviously it is not the accompanying historical events but the super-temporal redemptive work of God in the sacrifice of Golgotha which is thus continually brought into the present moment?

The supreme task of church art is to serve the liturgy. Hence church art is determined by a particular purpose. The building and furnishing of the House of God are subordinate to that purpose. But this subordination is the very reverse of a restriction or hampering of creative power. It is not so much a matter of subordination as of integration into the great reality of God's dealings with man.

The liturgy is primarily the representation—a representation in which the reality itself is present—of that Divine commerce. The ineffable and unfathomable mystery of the Incarnation of God is mysteriously continued in the liturgy. As with the Incarnation, it is a presence of God which is at once visible and invisible. Under the pitifully inadequate forms of earthly reality, there is enacted the epiphany of "the goodness and kindness of God our Saviour" (Tit. 3, 4). It is to serve the effect of this inrush of Divine reality, at once visible and veiled, that we have the ceremonies of the liturgy. And since the setting and arrange-

50

ment of the cult form part of its ceremonies, they have the same high purpose. The functional quality of church art is the measure of its lofty significance.

This profound and essential connection between the spiritual and the architectural House of God is given verbal expression when the same names are used for both: the House of God, the Church (= the house which belongs to the Lord), the Ecclesia—église, chiesa— (= the assembly of the elect) and the Temple (= the house set apart from the world). The church is the cult-place of the people of God, the house for the divine service of the Church.

The historical origin of the Christian church is the supper-room at Jerusalem. There the Lord Himself celebrated, as the origin and pattern for all time, the Eucharist which is the centre and heart of the Church's worship. Its continuation is the primary object of every church that is built. This function certainly does not necessitate any particular style of building; but the chief measure of the value of a church must be the degree to which it fulfils this function. To come down to concrete matters, we have no need to contrast basilicas with Gothic cathedrals to the disadvantage of either, or to insist on a centralised as against a longitudinal plan or vice versa. It is only possible to judge in the concrete whether a particular church is a valid setting for the Christian cult. The liturgical renewal taking place in our own day has made this essential matter the central point of its efforts in the field of church building. Modern church architecture, in its efforts to achieve interiors which shall be broad rather than long (cf. the latest Swiss churches), seems to be on the road to an ideal solution; a solution which will do justice both to the unchanging essence of a church and to the legitimate aspirations of our time. The desire to unite the congregation as closely as possible with what is going on at the altar necessarily involves paying closer attention to the problem of providing a special place on a smaller scale for smaller congregations (at week-day Mass, etc.). The tradition of the Church shows her to have been always ready to give the spirit of the age plenty of scope in the matter of church building. So there is nothing strange in the fact that we can see the aspirations of our time mirrored in its church architecture: its longing for primitive, authentic reality, for genuine simplicity, for community, for brightness and lightness, for open space and ordered clarity and the warmth and intimacy of a safe shelter.

This strong emphasis on the primary thing—the church as the setting for the celebration of the Eucharist—involves no neglect or repression of the church's other functions. It has also to be the setting for the administration of the other sacraments, for the adoration of the Sacrament of the Altar, for other devotions and for private prayer and meditation. The point is, that these different needs should be met in an orderly fashion. "Orderly" does not imply merely superficial practicality; it means rather that these different activities should be treated according to their essential significance. To take the last in our list as an example:

51

it would be fatal if, in our anxiety to make church building concentrate upon essentials, we should come to deny private prayer its right to be at home in the church. The man of today has even greater need than earlier generations of silence and recollection for the growth of his spiritual life, and he can seldom find them in his own home; provision for this must neither be neglected nor treated as a mere concession to an inferior level of piety. The apportionment of the interior of the church in accordance with this "sacred order" of things will be discussed in more detail later on. Let it suffice here to remark that the location of the place of our rebirth, of the forgiveness of sins, of the preaching of the gospel, of the choir and the organ, etc., is not a matter of indifference. Nor should their design be left at the mercy of merely subjective preferences or pragmatic considerations.

Nor is there anything irrelevant in building a house for the priest, the sacristan, the parish nuns, the parochial office and library, a house of hospitality or other buildings for charitable purposes in close association with the church; for the altar in the church is the centre, source and goal of all these things.

St. Thomas Aquinas says of the church as a building, "Domus ecclesiam significat," "The house (of God) signifies the Church" (Summa Theologica III, 83, 3). The church as a building is an image of the Church as the body of Christ. The mystical body of Christ: that means both the Head and the body, our Lord and His society. This we see set forth in the House of God: the altar signifies Christ, and the fabric of the church, made of innumerable stones all knit together, represents all His members. This image ought to be given clear and striking expression by the position and aspect of the altar as the dominating feature of the whole building.

But however much we may sing the praises of the beauty and glory of the House of God, it still remains a transitory building doomed to eventual destruction. And in this too it is a symbol of the living House of God. For the people of God, like its forerunner in the Old Testament, is still on the way, still wandering through the deserts of time to the Promised Land of the eternal and perfect Kingdom of God. And as the glory of the Lord was then truly present "in the Tent," so it is now present in the "Tent" of the church, though in a deeper and richer way. The word tabernacle (= tent) has preserved the memory of this relationship. The meaning of this as referring to the special place where the consecrated gifts are reserved applies fundamentally to the whole structure of the church: it is the Tent of God. The element of precariousness and insufficiency implied in this image will at last, when the day of the New Creation dawns, be swallowed up in the visible glory of the Lord. Then the people of God will no longer have any need of a cult-place, for they will themselves have become wholly the "Tent of God," the "City of God," "the new and eternal Jerusalem." But so long as the Church is still on her pilgrimage, she still builds her house of

52

stones and sees it, full of hope, as the image of that promise to which the word of God itself bears witness: "Behold the tabernacle of God with men; and he will dwell with them. And they shall be his people; and God himself with them shall be their God" (Apoc. 21, 3).

THE ALTAR

The altar is "the table of the Lord" (1 Cor. 10, 21), the "holy table" as it is still called in the Eastern liturgy, the table upon which the Lord, through the ministry of His servants, prepares the royal wedding-feast for His guests. From it He feeds us with the "bread of life" and the "drink of salvation." Upon it takes place the Pasch of the new people of God, the "passage of the Lord," for it is, as St. John Chrysostom says, "the table which bears the Lamb"; and so it is the stone of sacrifice upon which the cult represents the sacrifice of the "Lamb of God" for the reconciliation and deliverance of the faithful. It is the "high place" *(altare)* to which our Lord constantly returns to effect the meeting of God and man; where God stoops down from heaven to earth in sheer self-giving, and the Church offers earth up to heaven; where, in a word, the wonderful "exchange" takes place between God and man. Besides this function of being the place of the sacrifice and of the sacramental meal, the altar has a deep symbolic meaning. Its interpretation, going back to the fourth century, is given by the bishop in his address at the conferring of the subdiaconate: "Holy Church's altar is Christ Himself, as St. John testifies in his Apocalypse, when he says that he saw a golden altar standing before the Throne upon which and by which the offerings of the faithful are brought to the Father." It is difficult to analyse this symbolism more precisely, because of its manifold significance. For instance, the altar represents Christ as our Priest. For since our gifts and prayers ascend to God by means of the altar, and God's gifts come down to us on the altar, it is an image of Christ as the Mediator between God and man. Or, in another interpretation: since Christ becomes sacramentally present on the altar, the altar becomes the throne of the Lord; and since the throne is a sign of the ruler, the altar is a symbol of Christ. Or finally, Jesus is the Christ, the Anointed of the Holy Spirit, and since the altar is, at its dedication, anointed with chrism, it represents the true Anointed. What all these interpretations have in common is that they see this significance in the altar itself, without any addition, even of the tabernacle. Another thing common to them all is that the meaning of the altar cannot be read or seen from its shape but only from actions performed upon it. Hence it cannot be directly represented in the altar's structure. But how greatly it emphasises and underlines the unsurpassable dignity and holiness of the Christian altar. If we look on this symbolism not as a mere form of words but as the expression of a genuine reality, we shall come to understand the stress laid by the early Church on the importance of having only *one* altar in a place of worship. Eusebius gives to the altar the name of Christ, "the Only-begotten." The Eastern Church has never abandoned this principle. Before the sixth century, when side-altars began to appear in Western churches, an altar was always in its own separate chapel. The rise of private Masses in the early Middle Ages led to side-altars becoming more and more numerous and more and more taken for granted. Today, we still hear and read often enough that the altar represents Christ. If this truth is to be more than a merely intellectual notion, if it is to achieve visible expression, then care should be taken that, even if side-altars are a practical necessity, they are so arranged that the high altar clearly dominates the whole interior as its undoubted centre.

The Christological interpretation of the altar also sheds light on the meaning of the *sepulcrum* with its relics, which the Church requires in every altar. The saints are members of Christ. Their union with Christ is so intimate that it is expressed in an image which we can hardly grasp: they are "in Christ." They owe this being in Christ to the power which makes them holy. And the foundation of their holiness is, in a special way, the sacrifice of Christ. Seen in this way, there is a deep meaning in the presence in the altar of relics, earthly remains of the saints. Since the saints are "in Christ," it is fitting that their relics should be kept in the altar, the image of Christ.

The efforts being made in our time to keep the altar free from all unnecessary accretions do not represent a mere revival of an earlier style but a desire to do justice to the primitive significance of the altar. In the early ages, the altar held only those things which were needed for the Eucharistic sacrifice: the chalice of wine, the paten with the bread, the book, and the pyx to house the consecrated gifts. It was not till the Middle Ages that crosses[1] and candles began to be placed on the altar. Altar-pieces—retables, as they were called—arose from the custom of keeping and displaying relics on the altar. J. Braun, S.J., in *Der christliche Altar*, writes as follows of this development: "The reason why retables appear so late lies in the ancient, deeply-rooted custom of placing nothing on the altar except the holy vessels —chalice and paten—the sacred books, and the pyx with the Blessed Sacrament. It was based on the reverent awe in which the holiness and dignity of the altar were held. It was felt that, being the place where the holy sacrifice was offered, it should be reserved exclusively for that exalted purpose, and used for nothing else. Even the cross and candles were excluded from the altar itself. As late as the eleventh century, they are still normally placed behind the altar" (II, 542).

The altar must not be degraded to a substructure or pedestal. It is not there for the sake of its ornamentation—the ornament is there for the sake of the altar; the ornament must not develop independently, but in subordination to the meaning of the altar. It is a desecration of the altar when it is used as a cupboard for storing ornaments. Even to keep such things

[1] Thirteenth century: cf. Klauser, *Abendländische Liturgiegeschiechte*, p. 22.

54

behind the altar is a complete contradiction of the dignity of this "tremendous table," as St. John Chrysostom calls it. According to an official ecclesiastical ruling, an altar which contains a space in its structure for keeping vestments, vessels etc. may not be consecrated.[1] This exclusion of everything contradictory of the essential character of the altar does not apply to the canopy or baldachino. On the contrary, such a structure can contribute greatly to emphasising the dignity of the altar. It will, of course, only fulfill this function when it is unassumingly focussed on the altar, and not so designed and decorated as to draw attention to itself.

By its function and dignity the altar is the centre of holiness in the church. It is fitting that it should be somewhat withdrawn from the rest of the church and raised above it (which is the meaning of the word altar). Its function as the Eucharistic table of the sacrificial community requires that the interior of the church shall centre upon it. This truth— that it is the holy centre—does not imply that it must actually stand in the middle. However, it usually shows an inadequate realisation of this truth when the altar is placed in the apse immediately against the wall. From the point of view of the congregation, the altar must be placed in a position where "it can be seen by all" *(Instructio de arte sacra)*. J. Braun *(op. cit.* I, 407) says that it is "most fitting, most beautiful, and also most traditional" if the altar is placed in such a position that it can be freely approached from all sides. This is, in fact, positively required for the ceremony of consecrating the altar, which includes incensing it from all sides. Indeed, it is this full-scale incensing which is intended in our present abbreviated gesture at High Mass and Vespers. In addition, such a position for the altar is necessary if Mass is ever to be celebrated *versus populum*.

The question of the right place for the tabernacle is becoming a more and more important problem in the design of altars. Obviously we cannot give this complex question exhaustive treatment here. The more the Church becomes aware of the Eucharist as the act of the celebrant and congregation together, the more the problem arises. For if the celebrant stands behind the altar, facing the people, their common celebration of the liturgy becomes easier. Moreover, this position gives clearer expression to the idea that the priest is Christ's representative, sent "from above" to meet the congregation, whereas if he stands in front of the altar, with his back to the people of God, it suggests that he is there as their representative awaiting the coming of the Lord from the East. If we go back to the days when the communal celebration of Mass was taken for granted, we find no tabernacle problem. The early tradition against keeping the Sacrament on the altar where the liturgy was celebrated was so strong that it persisted into the Middle Ages and beyond, and even, in some countries, into

[1] Cf. Witte, *Das katholische Gotteshaus*, Mainz, 1951, p. 120, n. 8. A practical reference book on all questions of church building and furnishing. It can be recommended to all those who want information on the Church's rules and prescriptions in this field.

the nineteenth century; though by this time the faithful had mostly ceased to be active participants and become "silent spectators" (Pius XI in his Apostolic Constitution of 20th December 1928). Canon 1268 of the Code of Canon Law lays down directions for the reservation of the Eucharist, and the *Instructio de arte sacra* requires that attention be paid to it. The Eucharist "is to be kept in the most prominent and honourable place in the church, and hence normally on the High Altar, unless some other seems more suitable to the veneration and worship of so great a Sacrament. . . . But in cathedral, collegiate and conventual churches, where the Divine Office is celebrated at the High Altar, . . . the blessed Eucharist shall not, as a rule, be kept on the High Altar, but in a chapel or on some other altar." These directions are obviously intended to prevent any unworthy treatment of the Most Holy Sacrament, but they envisage the possibility that in some circumstances some other place might be found *commodius et decentius* for It, more suitable and fitting than the High Altar. We may hope that these words may be interpreted today in such a way as to do justice alike to the dignity of the Sacrament, ancient tradition, and the legitimate liturgical aspirations of our time.

It may be of interest that the *Caeremoniale Episcoporum,* the book containing the liturgical rules for bishops, includes the following instructions in this matter: "It is expedient that the Most Holy Sacrament should not be reserved on the High Altar nor on any other altar where the bishop or anyone else celebrates High Mass or Solemn Vespers" (1, 12, 8). "It would not be unsuitable, but on the contrary in the highest degree fitting, that at the altar where the Most Holy Sacrament is reserved, Mass should not be celebrated at all, this being, as we see, the ancient custom" (1, 12, 9).

THE SANCTUARY

The sanctuary exists for the sake of the altar. The whole of this area—also called the choir, from its former use—is entirely subordinated to the altar. This applies both to the way the whole space is laid out, and to the design of its individual details—altar-rails, east wall, windows, etc. When planning the sanctuary from an artistic point of view, this subordination to the altar and what takes place upon it must be reverenced as the ultimate law. The most important question here is that of the right place for the altar. It is determined by the altar's function as the Eucharistic table of the sacrificing community, as dealt with in the last chapter. The altar is *both* apart from the congregation *and* united with it, and in the same way it is not sufficient for the sanctuary simply to assert its separateness from the body of the church. The altar-rails—thought of nowadays chiefly as the communion-rail—fulfil this function of separation. But they must not in any way destroy the unity and community of the celebrant with his congregation. If they did, they would be contradicting

56

their own historical origins. There were altar-rails as far back as the fourth century, a time when communal participation in the celebration of Mass was taken completely for granted. Their principal function was seen then, and should be now, as the ensuring that only those people shall enter the sanctuary who are engaged in the service of the altar. It was seen, even at that early time, that they were also a suitable place at which to administer communion. But it was only when the passing of time had established the custom of receiving communion kneeling that they became a communion-rail in our modern sense. They are a help in the orderly distribution of the sacred Food, and also give the communicants something to lean on if they are old or infirm. The Church's law contains no instructions about their design.

In the interests of general participation in the liturgy, the sanctuary should not be too long, so as to keep the sacred actions in sight of the faithful; but it should not be so short as to cramp the performance of the ceremonies. The most important thing in it, after the altar, is the pulpit. Its ancient place was here, in the sanctuary, or more precisely at the meeting-place of sanctuary and nave. As late as the Middle Ages, the preacher would still sit to deliver his sermon. To be seated was looked upon as expressing authority. With churches growing bigger and bigger during the Middle Ages, and altars further and further away from the congregation, practical considerations led to placing the pulpit in the nave itself. Parallel with this came the gradual detachment of the sermon from the celebration of Mass. Our present movement back to essentials is leading to a restoration of the sermon to its place in the Mass. This is receiving architectural expression in the more and more frequent placing of ambos and pulpits at the altar-rails. Thus the pulpit comes back to proximity and relationship to the altar. It is the place of the proclamation of the word of God. Both word and sacrament come from the Lord. Our Lord feeds His people with the bread of God's word and the bread of His body. The altar is the table from which He provides this food. Hence there is a deep symbolism in having the same place for the communication of the word of the Lord as for the communication of the body of the Lord: it comes out from the altar at the altar rails.

The sermon itself is in process of change at the present time. Preachers today are becoming more and more conscious of the nature of preaching as the proclamation of God's message of salvation. The straight-forward, authentic fulfilment of this "service of the word" has become once again their primary object. Accordingly, any suggestion of Baroque ornamentation is completely alien to the modern pulpit. But a proper relation between design and function is not to be confused with lack of life and imagination; simplicity is not the same as crudity. There are no canonical stipulations concerning the structure of the pulpit.

57

We have recently been witnessing a reversal of the earlier historical process which first detached the *schola cantorum* from the ministry of the altar and then set the outward seal upon this separation by putting the choir in a gallery at the west end of the church. Today, any choir which is conscious of its religious function realises that it is not a kind of musical club but an official liturgical member of the sacrificial community. It follows that its true place is near the altar. And its task there is not to replace the singing of the congregation but to sing those parts of the liturgy which belong to it alone and otherwise to lead the congregational singing. It could have only a profoundly good and invigorating effect on the liturgy if organists, too, would become more aware of the official nature of their function. Here, too, the true line of development must lead away from everything in the nature of a concert performance and towards what is authentically liturgical. The right place for the organ is not so obvious as that for the choir. In cases where, for acoustical or other technical reasons, it is not possible to have the organ near the altar, it may at least be feasible to have the key-board, at any rate, near the choir.

The design of the east wall and its windows again needs to be subordinated to the action of the cult. They should not be left to the unrestricted whim of either the artist or the patron. They must avoid ostentation, so that the eye will rest not on them but on the altar. If they are adorned with images of any kind, then they must be chosen for their relation to the action of the cult and the essential work of salvation. Those which are not appropriate to the whole cycle of the Church's year should not be considered suitable for this wall. The liturgical text of the Mass is a rich source of suitable themes. Since the Eucharist is a *signum praefigurativum,* stress should be laid on images which herald the world to come. Much too little use is made of the great symbols and mysteriously significant images of the Apocalypse.

It is also perfectly possible to leave the wall completely plain, though this may seem a strange idea to most people today. But emptiness need not be merely negative; it may be a true and valid expression of the creature's humility before the invisible and inexpressible *tremendum mysterium.*

THE FONT

Apart from emergencies, baptism is administered in the baptistry. The font *(fons baptismalis,* the well-spring of baptism) is the place where a man is reborn "of water and the Holy Spirit" into the sonship of God and so into a new life of fellowship with God through His Son in the power of the Spirit. Here is sacramentally accomplished the death of the old man, the slave of sin, and the resurrection of the new. Since this death and resurrection take place through and in Christ, the person baptised is incorporated into the body of Christ,

58

His Church. Baptism is the sacrament of new beginning, and hence the *decens locus*, the "fitting place" for it of which the *Rituale Romanum* speaks is near the entrance to the church. It is a contradiction of the meaning of this most basic of sacraments to push the font away into some corner of the church. Nor does it correspond to the meaning of baptism to put it on the sanctuary. This last, when it is not simply a matter of convenience, is usually the result of a praiseworthy desire to keep the faithful vividly in mind of their baptism. But this advantage is won at the cost not merely of a diminution of the symbolic value of place but a total destruction of it, which hampers a right understanding of this first of the sacraments of the Church, called by the *Rituale Romanum* "the door to the Christian life and to eternal life." It accords with the nature of baptism that it should be administered near the entrance of the church. "The fitting *(decens)* place for the font, in the sense of the Roman ritual, is near the door of the church, either in the nave or in a chapel communicating with it. On no account should it be on the sanctuary, to which not even the baptised laity, let alone catechumens, are allowed access."[1] As a vivid reminder to the faithful of the meaning of the sacrament, the baptistry should be so placed that they cannot fail to see it whenever they come into church. It may be placed immediately inside the entrance. But it would bring out its meaning more strongly to put it in the porch, or in a separate baptistry communicating with the church. But whatever place is chosen for it, it should certainly be devoted exclusively to the meaning and celebration of baptism. To let any other devotion have its place here would be an offense against the dignity of the sacrament and would also weaken the symbolism of its setting. The arrangement and adornment of the baptistry should be visibly related to the inner effects of baptism. Here again we must stress that its whole design—especially where adorned with figures or symbols—must be determined by the essential character of the place. In particular, the font should not be a mere container for the baptismal water. It is sad to see that in many cases today this is in fact the only function the font has. The actual baptism is performed quite apart from it. And yet it is the place where baptism ought to be administered, for it is the *fons baptismalis,* the well-spring wherein man is cleansed by "the laver of regeneration" and introduced into a new life. We can only most earnestly hope that due regard will be had for this truth in the actual administration of baptism.

THE PORCH

Only with a heart well prepared can man take part in the mysteries of faith. Hence it is altogether astonishing to see the scanty attention which has hitherto been paid, despite the efforts of liturgists, to the idea of the porch in relation to the church.

[1] L. Eisenhofer, *Handbuch der Katholischen Liturgik,* 1932, Vol. I, p. 386.

What is accepted as indispensable for any theatre or concert-hall—an intermediate place where people can get themselves ready—is considered as unnecessary for a church. Yet if any building needed such a thing, it is surely the Lord's House. Every school of the spiritual life teaches the necessity of preparation as a condition for meeting God. Should not this fundamental truth be given structural expression, especially in an age when almost everything is busy helping man to distraction, and almost nothing to recollection? In country districts, the walk to church may still partly fulfil this purpose. But in towns it does the opposite. This especially affects the young. It is true that if the surroundings of the church are well planned they can be a helpful preparation. But the only adequate solution is an entrance-hall intentionally designed for the purpose. We need a modern version of the early Christian atrium and the mediaeval "paradise." The few tentative efforts made so far have not achieved their goal.

An open porch is not enough. If it is to fulfil its function of release and recollection, it must be generously proportioned. But an entrance hall of this sort could fulfil other purposes as well: it could contain the parish notice-board, the book-stall, holy water stoups and shrines for private devotion. The baptistry could be designed as part of it.

Are we still too far in advance of the times in trying at least to suggest the idea of making the porch into a real hall on these lines; and of including in it a chapel for confessions—a place for "the toilsome baptism," as the early Church called the sacrament of penance?

PICTURES AND STATUES

Images within the cult-place of the Christian Church are to be "signs of faith": no more, but no less. This faith does not refer to a subjective seeking after or apprehension of religious things, of whatever degree of integrity or intensity. Its reference is to the objective world of divine mystery, attainable only by revelation: the coming of the Kingdom of God, which means the reign of God and the salvation of man. Is it not an impossible undertaking, or even blasphemous presumption, to attempt to embody this in a work of art? For we are here concerned with the actions of God, the invisible, incomprehensible, unimaginable, of whom the Scriptures bear witness, even in the New Testament, that He "inhabiteth light inaccessible: whom no man hath seen, nor can see" (1 Tim. 6, 16). If even to speak of Him is governed by the paradoxes of the prophetical and apostolic office, to make any visual representation of the *tremendum mysterium* would seem to be a sheer impossibility. Then was not Old Testament piety more profoundly and reverently wise than we in its approach to the mystery of God, when in obedience to God's word (Exodus 20, 4-6) it excluded any representation of God in an image? And are not certain Christian bodies, by prohibiting images, expressing a more humble faith than that expressed by all the unnum-

60

berable self-assured, and all too often self-satisfied, images of the Divine Reality in our churches? So long as we are at the level of human ability and human effort, all such attempts are indeed condemned from the start as futile and forbidden. Yet from her earliest days the Church has regarded the Incarnation of God as making a pictorial representation of the work of redemption both possible and justified. Jesus Christ is "the image of the invisible God" (Col. 1, 15). In Him God has taken human form and become visible. He Himself bears witness of the degree to which the Hidden God has come into the visible world in this "image": "He that seeth me seeth the Father also" (John 14, 9). In His Son, who is the Word and the Image of God, God has come forth from His hiddenness. And this fact— coming from God Himself—is what makes it possible to "illustrate" the divine mystery in images for the understanding of the faithful. But we must not misunderstand the nature of this visible action of God and the resulting possibility of its representation in art. In and after the Incarnation, God remains the Hidden God. Whatever may be revealed of His acts and His will, He Himself remains "in light inaccessible." The mystery of the Kingdom of God is under a veil. As God in the earthly life of His son remains ultimately hidden and invisible, and as in the cult which the Church celebrates the redeeming work of God is made present at once visibly and invisibly, so the maker of images must not presume to suppose that he can make a visual representation of God Himself. The Council of Trent in its seventieth session requires that the people be instructed that "images are not made of the God-head as though to suggest that It can be seen with the eyes of the body or made visible in colour and shape."

Images should be in the service of the word. The task of both is to set forth Jesus Christ before our eyes (Gal. 3, 1). The word of the gospel, as the theologians tell us, is analogical speech, i.e. speech in which the dissimilarity between the divine and the earthly reality is greater than the similarity. The principle of analogy applies even more strongly to works of art. "The being of God, as He is in Himself, is unknowable by us in this life. But we can know Him as imaged in the perfections of creation" *(Summa Theologica* I, 13, 2 ad 3). This sentence of St. Thomas Aquinas is confirmed, not contradicted, by the images present in the faith itself. But if it does not make nonsense of the preaching of the Good News, neither can we conclude from it that the application of art to these matters is impossible.

An image is to be a "sign of faith." It cannot represent "what it is really like." And, on the other hand, it is more than a merely naturalistic representation of an historical event. Whether it is an image of Christ or an image of a saint, it is always a "sign." It does not stop short at the natural event, but points beyond it to the mystery at work in it. Its essential task is to be transcendent. Hence these images of faith are not honoured for their own sake but for the sake of that reality to which they refer.

61

The Council of Trent makes the matter of the reverence due to images of Christ and the saints unmistakably clear. "They are to be shown the honour and reverence due to them, not as though it were believed that there dwells in them any divinity or power for which they are to be honoured; nor as though it were possible to ask them for anything; nor as though we put our trust in images, like the pagans who hoped in idols; but because the reverence shown them is directed to that which they represent. So when we kiss images, take off our hats to them or kneel to them, we are adoring Christ and honouring the saints whom they represent."[1]

A work of art reaches the level of true witness only when it aims at being a sign of faith and nothing else. Its witness will be effective in the measure that it is rooted in a reverent recognition of the limits of artistic creativity and an overwhelming sense of the inadequacy of all human powers of conception before the reality of God.

Images in church are meant, then, to be at the service of the preaching of the faith. This immensely high task requires the artist to submit his creative action to the judgment of the word of God. His uncontrolled subjectivity and creative fantasy must be disciplined by faith. Since he is being called to be a witness to the truth through his work, he will not regard it as a restriction of his freedom when the Church exercises her pastoral office and refuses to have images inside the church which contradict truths of faith (cf. Canon 1279 of the Code of Canon Law). This ordinance is not concerned with aesthetic questions of style and form. In these, so long as no offense is offered to the dignity and holiness of the faith, the artist is free. The prohibition (Canon 1279, 1) against setting up any "unusual image" in the church must be understood in the Church's traditional sense, which means that "unusual" applies to the Church's doctrine and not to matters of style.

The divine mystery follows an intelligible order in its unfolding. The Church's preaching, whose task is to declare and explain it, must conform to this same order. Hence it must also be the measure of the making of images. No indifference can attach to the question of what is displayed in a church, nor to that of where the emphasis is placed in the choice of themes. Preaching is today concentrating more than ever on the teaching of the central mysteries of the faith, and the same demand for the essential core of the history of the redemption must have a determining effect on the images with which the church is adorned. Hence Pius XII, in his encyclical *Mediator Dei* of November 20th, 1947, considers it his duty to "reprove the ill-educated piety which, in churches intended for the worship of God, and even on the altars, displays for veneration an unreasonable multiplicity of pictures and statues; . . . and which insists on unimportant trifles while neglecting what is important and necessary. This is to hold religion up to ridicule and cheapen the dignity of divine worship."

[1] Neuner-Roos, *Der Glaube der Kirche*, 1938, no. 402.

Perhaps, after the neglect of the last few centuries, this new sense of values may lead to a fresh awareness of the typological significance of Old Testament figures and events—Noe, Abraham, Melchisedech, Jonas, Daniel, the youths in the fiery furnace, etc.

This law of concentration applies in particular to the wall behind the High Altar, at which the faithful must constantly be looking. This is the place for the great themes of the mystery of Christ. It should be devoted to those events in our Lord's life which especially reveal Him as God or as Saviour (e.g. the adoration of the Magi, the Baptism in Jordan, the Transfiguration, the Resurrection, the Parousia, the King-Shepherd, the Kyrios). Ideally, this is the place for images which have a reference both to the cult and to the end of time—a condition fulfilled in these examples, in some more plainly and in some in a more veiled manner. Their pointing simultaneously to past events in the story of salvation, to their present reality in the cult, and to their final fulfilment at the end of time makes them "signs of faith" in the fullest sense. If any images of saints appear here, they must be of such a kind as to show plainly that these are men who are members of Christ, and the source of whose holiness is precisely that membership.

In addition to this stress on essentials, it is important that the various statues in a church should have some intelligible relationship to each other. Their selection and arrangement are not matters to be left to the private preferences and whims of the priest or lay-patron, nor of the artist either. What we see in practice at present is almost always a complete lack of plan and integration. This is no help in the task, so important today, of giving the faithful an informed faith, with a true grasp of essentials; on the contrary, it encourages the fragmentation of religious ideas already prevailing in the minds of the people.

God who is truth is also absolute beauty. That He is utterly *other*, and therefore incomprehensible, applies equally to God's beauty, the splendour of His truth and His being. It transcends every human power of imagination or representation. The supreme achievements of art remain only a shadow of the reality. But to conclude from this that artistic quality is of minor relevance in the realm of the faith and its proclamation comes near to blasphemy. The same claim is made on the artist for beauty as for truth. But this beauty reflecting the being of God is not of course to be confused with any particular ideal of beauty as represented by some particular style. There is no need, for instance, to canonise that kind of harmonious sweetness which gratifies the senses of the beholder. Images which are "signs of faith" will rather tend to burst asunder the limits and repose of this world's beauty.

Sentimental trash, lying outside the field of art altogether, is the enemy of faith. It is a practical denial of the unity of truth and beauty in God. It makes the faith the laughing-stock of unbelievers, sets obstacles in the way of those who are seeking it, and does not

63

merely ruin the *taste* of the faithful but works against any true reverence and awe of the unimaginable greatness and immensity of the realities of the faith. In a word, it debases and degrades the faith. Hence the *Instructio de arte sacra* condemns trash in churches in the plainest terms.

The ninety-fifth psalm says, "Praise and beauty are before him: holiness and majesty in his sanctuary." To bear witness to the mighty reality and exalted beauty of God, so far as they are reflected in His earthly works, is the function of images in the Church.

ILLUSTRATIONS

Karl Moser: Church of St. Antony, Basel, 1927.

Auguste Perret: Church of St. Thérèse at Montmagny near Paris, 1925.

Auguste Perret: Notre Dame du Raincy, Paris; interior, looking towards the altar, 1922.

Fritz Metzger: Church of St. Charles Borromeo, Lucerne, 1933.

Hermann Baur: St. Michael's,
Hirzbrunnen, Basel;
the main entrance,
seen from the Almendstrasse,
with the baptistry on the right.

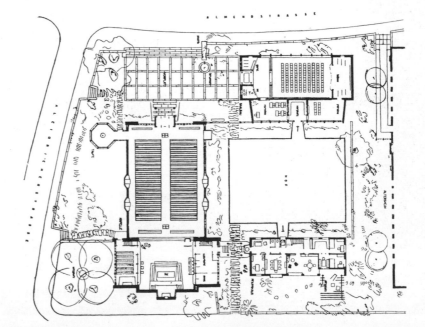

7

Fritz Metzger: Church of Our Lady of Lourdes, Seebach (Zürich), 1935.
Below: the exterior. Above: drawing of the interior by Richard Seewald, showing his murals.
Such pictures of Our Lady are not altogether appropriate in the sanctuary itself (see text).

Fritz Metzger: Church of SS. Felix and Regula, Zürich, 1950.

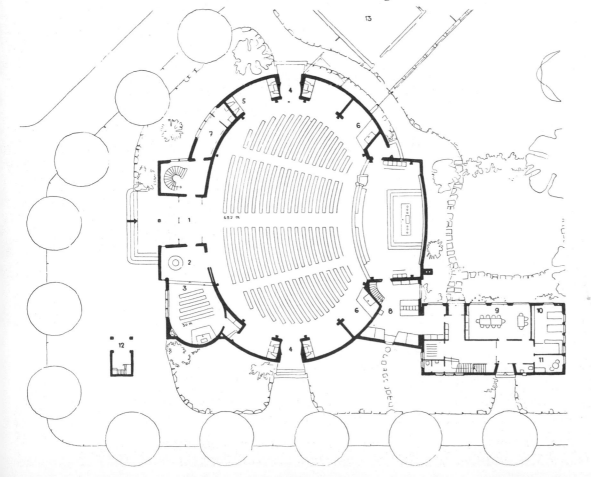

Plan:
1 Main Entrance.
2 Baptistry.
3 Chapel for
week-day use.
4 Side entrances.
5 Confessionals.
6 Side altars.
7 Cloak room.
8 Sacristy.
9, 10, 11 Pres-
bytery.
12 Tower.
13 Parish hall.

9

Fritz Metzger: St. Francis, Riehen, Switzerland, with its surroundings.

Plan:
1 Baptistry, entrance and porch.
2 Sanctuary.
3-4 Pulpits.
5 Sacristy.
6 Chapel for week-day use.
7 Confessionals.
8 Bell tower.
9 Rectory.
10 Parish hall.

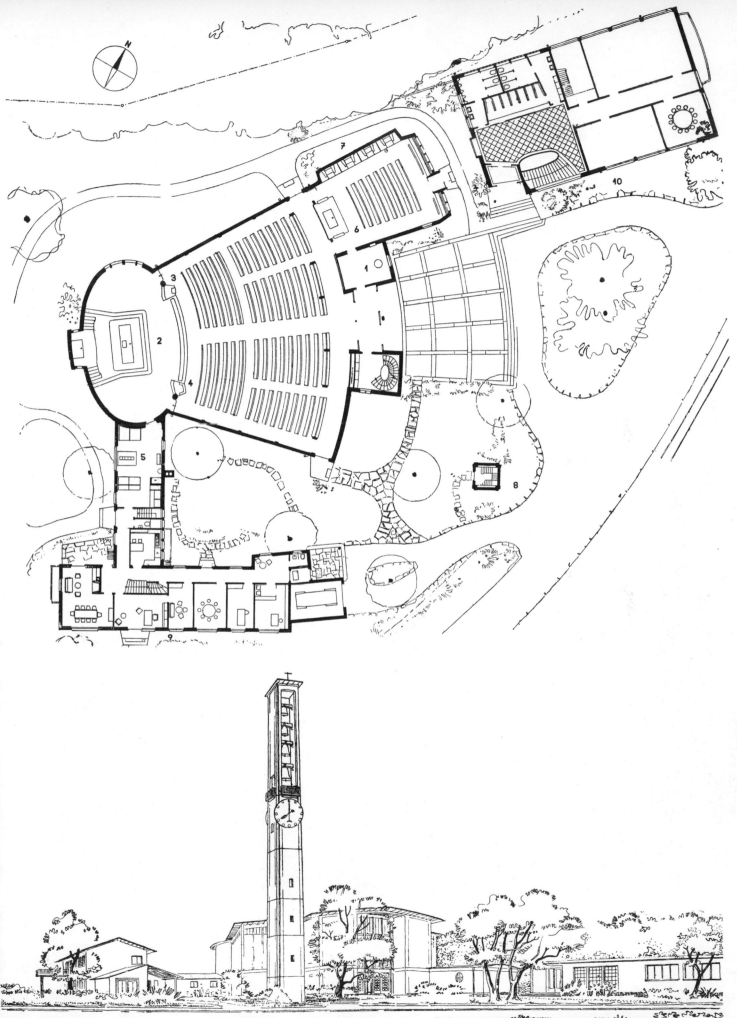

Henri Matisse: Dominican convent chapel at Vence, 1951.

Jean Lurçat: Tapestry in church at Assy.

Novarina and Malot: Church at Assy, 1945-47; natural basalt stone.

Hans Schädel: St. Alfonsus Church, Würzburg.

Le Corbusier: Chapel of Notre Dame du Haut, Ronchamp;
exterior showing pulpit for outdoor ceremonies.

Burlage and Niebuer: St. Joseph's, Greven, Westphalia. The basic idea was to
make the sanctuary a laminated enclosure, corresponding to the beamed roof.

18

Rudolf Schwarz: Church of the Assumption, Wesel, 1951-52.
Above: looking towards the altar.
Below: looking towards the west wall.

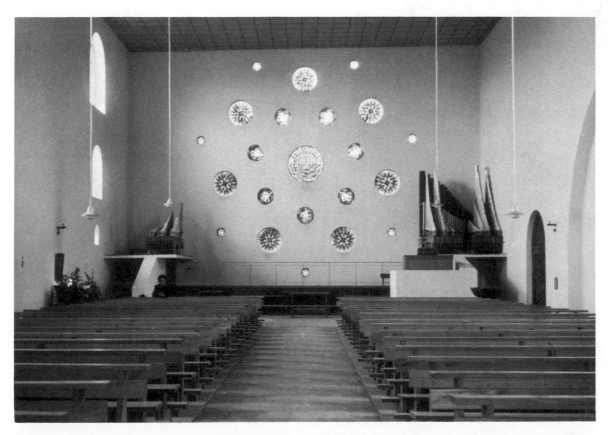

M. Novarina: Church of the Sacred Heart, Audincourt, France. Mosaic by
Jean Bazaine. Same church; interior. Windows of glass blocks in cement
and altar background by Fernand Léger.

Church of the Sacred Heart, Audincourt, France: One of a series of glass block windows by Fernand Léger illustrating the instruments of the Passion.

Dominikus Böhm: St. Engelbert's, Riehl; view of the altar. The bold arches of the concrete vault spring from ground level.

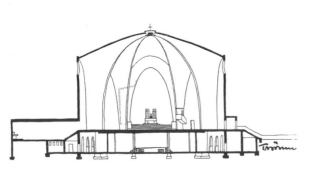

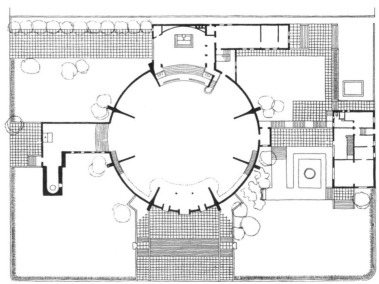

Dominikus Böhm: St. Engelbert's, Riehl; exterior.

View of the altar. Note the light, airy, tent-like construction.

Dominikus Böhm: Church for summer visitors at Norderney.
A view of the entrance-porch and bell-tower.

Enrique de la Mora: La Purisima Church, Monterrey, Mexico.

La Purisima Church interior.

Emil Steffann: Franciscan church at Cologne. An interior resulting from partial
modern reconstruction of the surviving ruins on the old plan.

Emil Steffann: Reconstruction of the neo-Gothic choir of the Franciscan church at Cologne. The remaining part of the building, with its historicist character, blends successfully with a modern design.

Hans Schädel: St. Kilian's, Schweinfurt, 1953.

Dominikus and Gottfried Böhm: St. Antony's, Münster, 1951.
A modern interior in a burnt-out neo-Baroque shell.

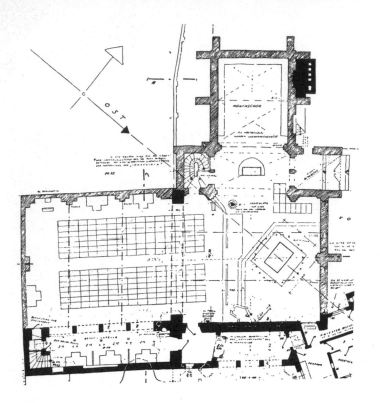

Emil Steffann: Franciscan church, Cologne (see pp. 28-29).

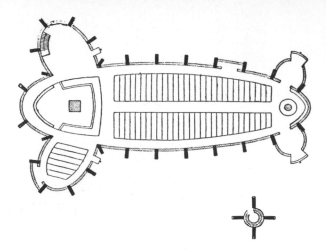

Rudolf Schwarz: St. Michael's, Frankfurt, 1954.

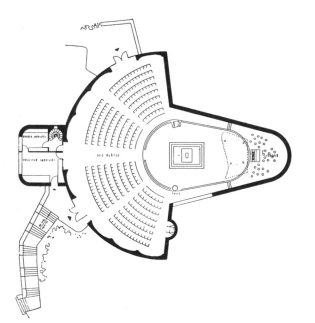

Hans Schilling: Plan for the Church of
the Holy Angels, Wesel.

Alfons Leitl: St. Sebastian's, Aachen, 1953.

Though so different from each other,
all these plans illustrate the aim
of emphasizing the brotherhood of the
congregation gathered round the
altar, and the altar itself as the
unquestionable focal point of the
whole church.

Hans Schädel:
Plan for the
church at
Kleinheubach.

Hans Schwippert: Reconstruction of St. Engelbert's, Mülheim, Ruhr, 1952-53. The altar, a plain table, is set slightly above the nave level. Altar, ambo, communion rails and benches all form a properly planned unity. Only the walls of the neo-Gothic church (1901) remained; pillars and roof had been destroyed. Above stucco ceiling is a steel frame resting on very slender supports; steel tubes tapering towards the base.

Henri Matisse: The altar of the Dominican convent chapel at Vence (see pp. 12 and 13).

Chasuble designed by Henri Matisse.

Rudolf Schwarz and Hans Warnecke: Altar with tabernacle, monstrance, sanctuary lamp and candles; Church of Christ the King, Fulda, 1939.

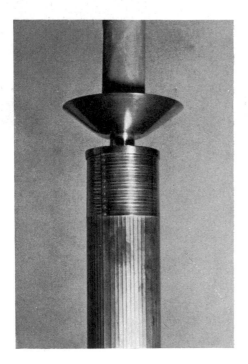

Albert Schilling: Altar of the Church of All Saints, Neubad (Basel), 1950.

Albert Schilling: Relief behind the altar at Möhlin: the Lamb of the Apocalypse;
shell limestone (14 ft., 4 ins. x 10 ft., 9 ins.), 1950.

Below: Albert Schilling: Carving on the altar of St. Michael's, Hirzbrunnen, jurassic limestone
(7 ft., 2 ins. x 2 ft., 6 ins.). Emblems of the Blessed Eucharist (host and fish), with a seraph in
adoration.

Rudolf Schwarz: Adaptation of the Church of Our Lady, Trier. A successful treatment of an old church of great architectural beauty.

Hein Wimmer and Rudolf Schwarz: Baldachino and altar of the Blessed Sacrament in the Church of Our Lady. T-shaped cross in Indian ebony bound with silver, silver figure. Altar in grey sandstone. Baldachino of gilded bronze resting on stone columns.

Josef Jaeckel: Chalice; iron base, figure spun-cast in silver, ivory node, cup silver, interior gilt.

Hein Wimmer: Silver chalice; base silver, with design in niello; crystal node, gilt cup.

Elisabeth Treskow: Chalice; silver cup, base silver-plated.

Hein Wimmer: Silver-gilt chalice; enamelled knobs on node, engraved inscription.

Hein Wimmer: Silver-gilt ciborium; enamel handle (pattern of ears of corn), engraved frieze of fishes, crystal knob.

Fritz Schwerdt: Communion-paten.

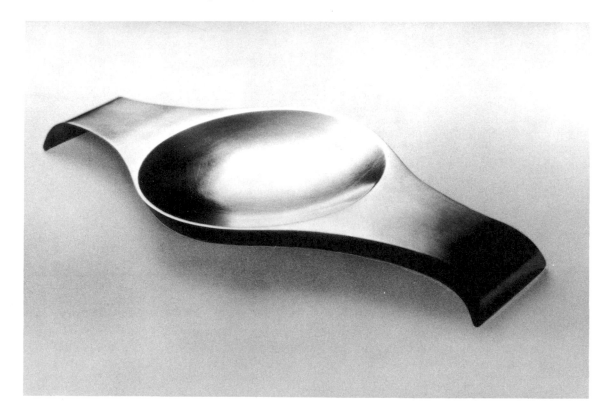

Hein Wimmer: Silver-gilt ciborium with crystal cross.

Hein Wimmer: Pyx and burse for sick-calls.

School of Arts and Crafts, Krefeld: Plate for the offertory-procession; silver-plated copper and ebony.

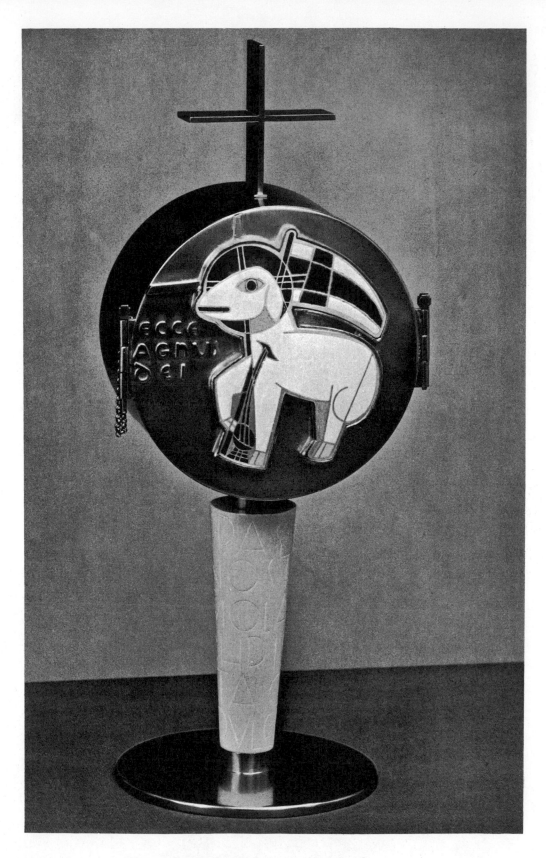

Hein Wimmer: Pyx; silver gilt, with enamelled lamb;
shaft, ivory with carved inscription.

Hein Wimmer: Monstrance; silver gilt, cross set with topazes, disk in turquoise-blue enamel with symbolic figures: pelican, eagle, lion, griffin=love, resurrection, kingship, God-man; engraved inscription at base.

Karl Schrage: Silver cruets.

Th. A. Winde:
Boxes for hosts,
in oak.

51

Fritz Schwerdt: Altar candlestick in nickel-plated brass.

Hein Wimmer: Altar candlestick in bronze and crystal.

Hein Wimmer: Sanctuary lamp.

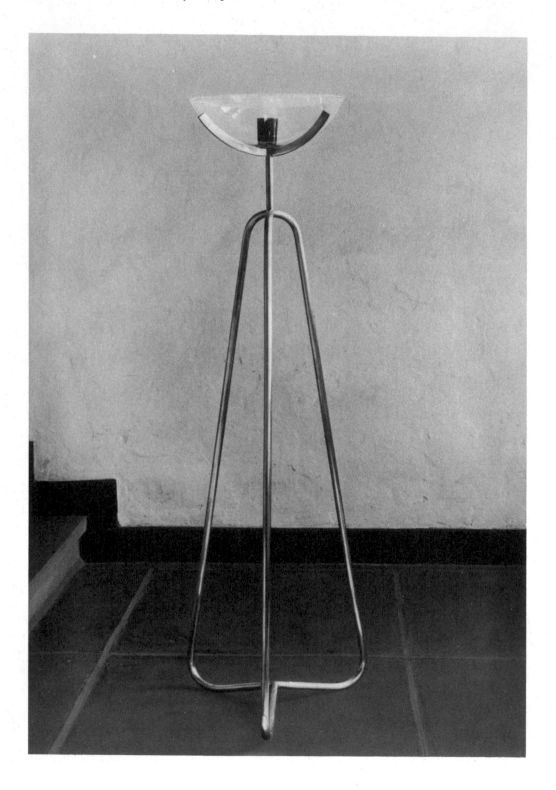

Hein Wimmer: Silver baptismal vessels.

Emil Steffan and H. G. Bücher: Baptismal font in St. Boniface Church in Dortmund.

Albert Schilling: The font in St. Michael's,
Hirzbrunnen (Basel); jurassic limestone, diameter 4 ft.

Dominikus Böhm: Font in St. Wolfgang's, Regensburg, in Kelheim limestone; bronze cover by Hans Rheindorf, with the symbols of the four evangelists.

Hein Wimmer: Font in volcanic basalt, with bronze cover.

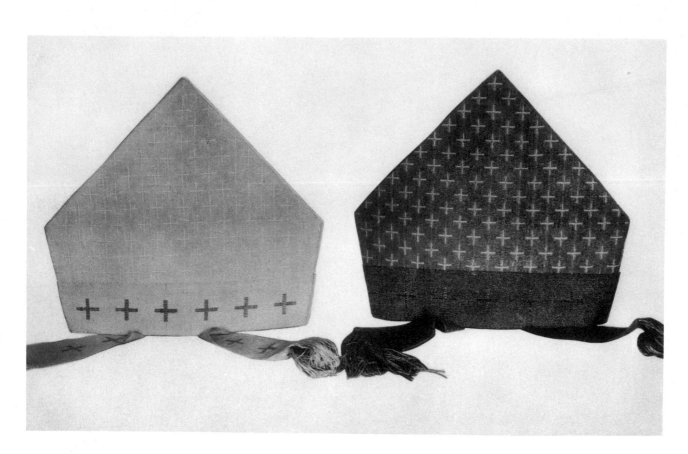

Hans Dinnendahl: Mitres, hand woven by Klara Keuffer.

Karl Schrage:
Bishop's ring.

Elisabeth Treskow: Detail of crozier: the baptism of Christ. Silver decorated with gold; figures cast and chased, dove embossed in gold.

M. Augustina Flüeler: Chasuble.

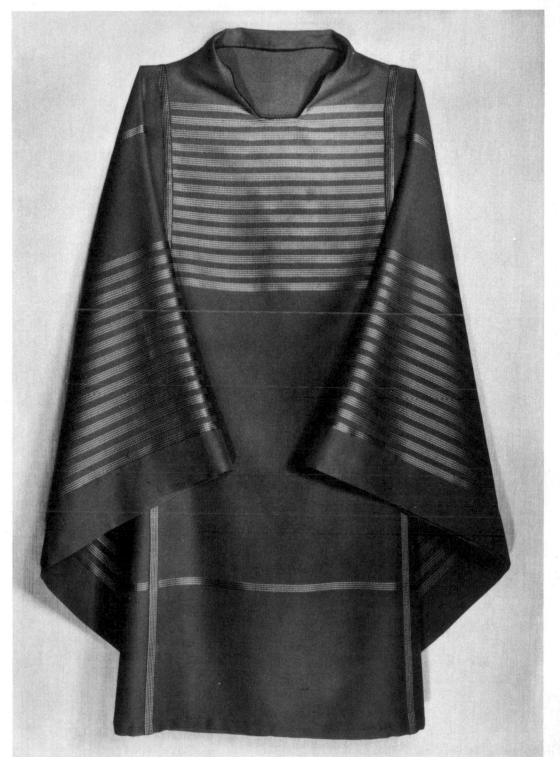

M. Augustina Flüeler:
Red dalmatic.

M. Augustina Flüeler: Chasuble and stole.

M. Augustina Flüeler: Chasuble.

M. Augustina Flüeler: Chasuble and stole.

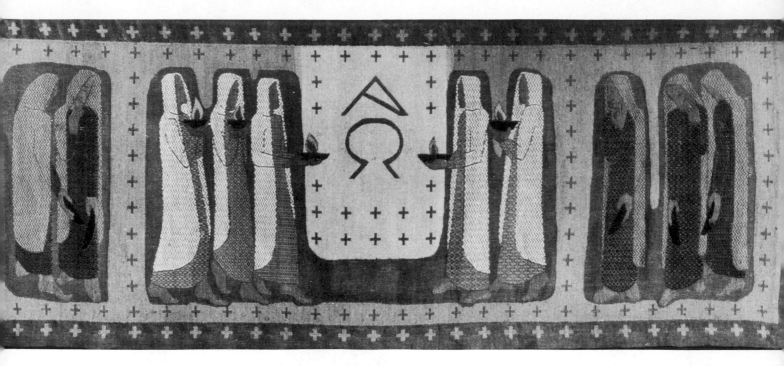

Else Mögelin: Tapestry of the wise and foolish virgins.

Lydia Jungmann:
Cloth for a
baptismal candle,
embroidered in
white.

Toni Schneider-Manzell:
Baptismal candlestick
in bronze.

Ernst Barlach: Crucifix for St. Elizabeth's, Marburg.

Kurt Schwippert: Crucifix with bronze figure, 7½ ins. high.

Gerhard Marcks: Crucifix with bronze figure, 1 ft., 11 ins. high.

Paul Mersmann: Annunciation.

Ewald Mataré: Man of Sorrows.

Hilde Schürk-Frisch:
Madonna; bronze,
5 ft., 2 ins. high. (Right)

Edwin Scharff: Detail from the door at Marienthal near Wesel, 1950: "Creator of Heaven and Earth"; "Rose Again From the Dead"; "Descended Into Hell"; "The Forgiveness of Sins."

Edwin Scharff: Church door at Marienthal near Wesel, 1950; bronze. The creed in
pictorial emblems, linked by a continuous ribbon.

Ernst Barlach: Hovering angel; formerly at Güstrow, now in the memorial church
of the Minorites at Cologne.

Vincenz Pieper: Detail from the design for a window in Cologne Cathedral: the Prophet Isaias.

Anton Wendling:
Symbol of an evangelist.

Georges Rouault: Man of Sorrows, Assy, 1939.

Jacob Epstein:
Madonna and Child;
cast lead. London.

81

Günther Peltzer: Details of a church window.

Ludwig Baur:
Patronal window,
St. Peter's,
Recklinghausen.

Georg Meistermann: East window in St. Kilian's, Schweinfurt, 1953 (see p. 30).

Karl Schrage: Censer, incense-boat and spoon.

Hein Wimmer: Censer, incense-boat and spoon.

Lambert Rucki: Cocks; often used on church steeples.

Lambert Rucki: Pietà.

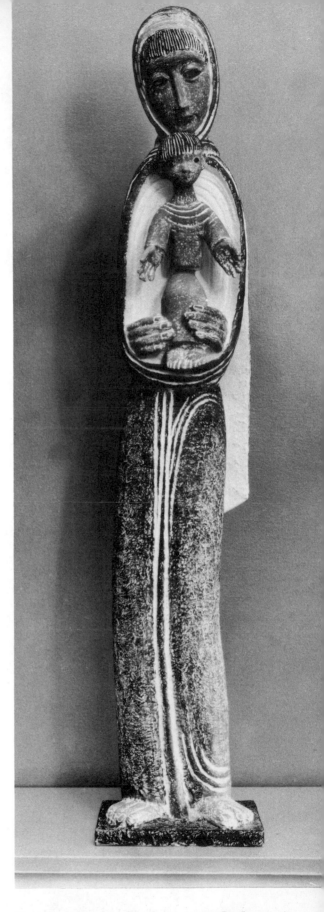

Lambert Rucki: Madonnas (polychrome).

Suzanne Nicolas: Station of the Cross; cast stone; Saint Joseph's Abbey, Spencer, Massachusetts.

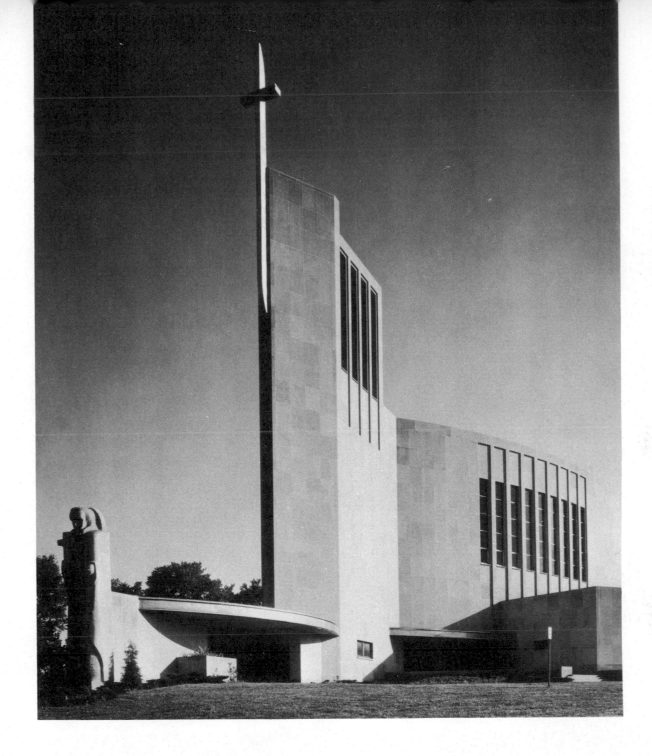

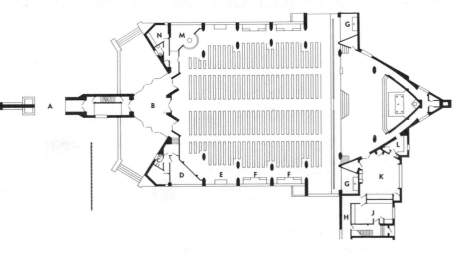

Barry Byrne, architect:
Church of St. Francis Xavier,
Kansas City, Missouri.

Barry Byrne, architect: Church of St. Columba, St. Paul, Minnesota.

Church of St. Columba; interior.

Murphy and Mackey, architects: Church of the Resurrection of Our Lord, St. Louis, Missouri.

Church of the Resurrection
of Our Lord; interior.
Note location of Baptistry.

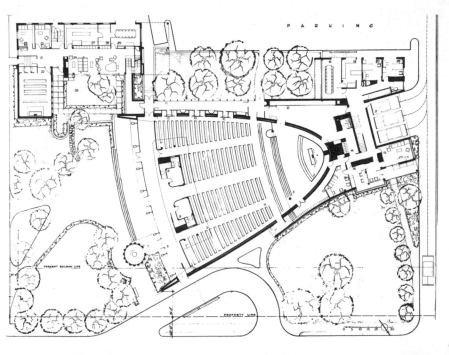

Murphy and Mackey, architects: Church of St. Peter, Kirkwood, Missouri.

Church of St. Peter;
interior and plan.

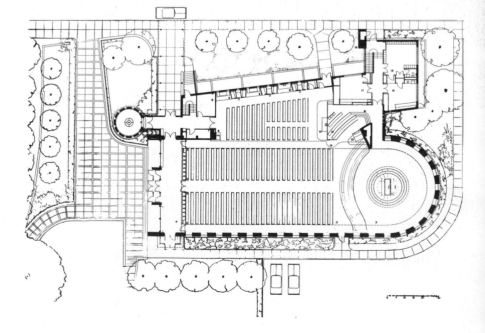

Chaix and Johnson, architects: St. Brigid's Church, Los Angeles, California.

St. Brigid's Church; interior.

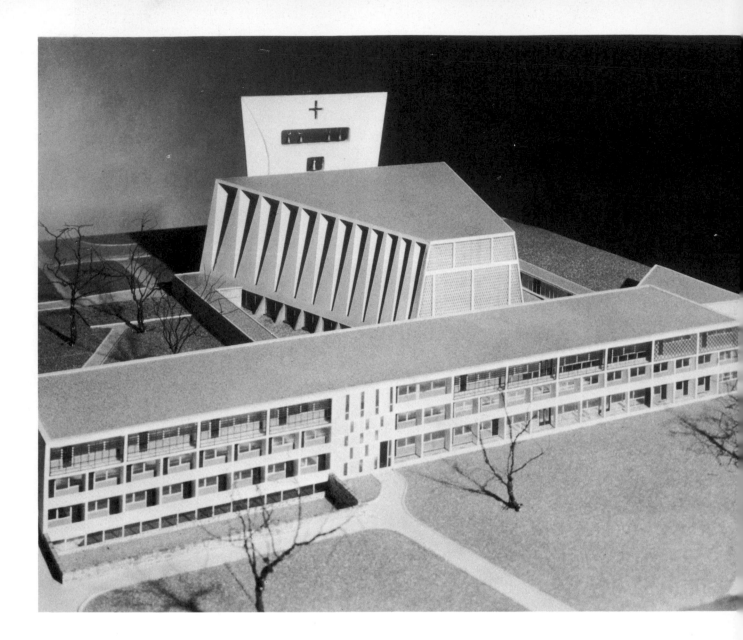

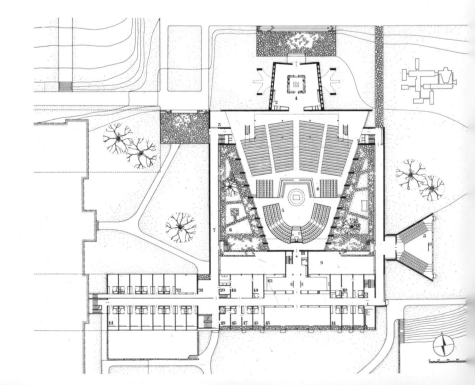

Marcel Breuer, architect:
St. John's Abbey,
Collegeville, Minnesota.
The monastic wing is the first
building constructed to date.

Paul Thiry; Fox and Ballas, architects: Church of St. Anthony, Missoula, Montana.

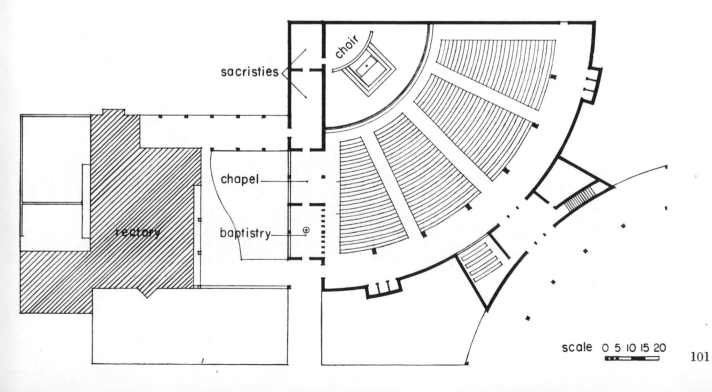

Chaix and Johnson, architects: St. Albert's Church, Compton, California.

William R. Burk and Associates, architects: Pius X Church and School, New Orleans, Louisiana.

Elsa Schmid: Phoenix; mosaic fresco.

Louisa Jenkins: Mosaic.

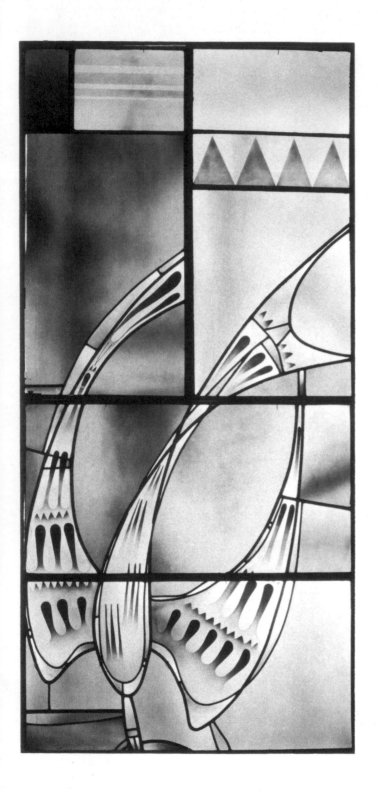
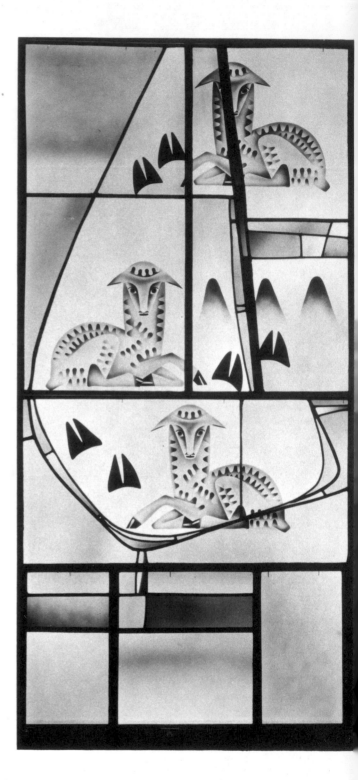

Emil Frei: Windows representing the Holy Ghost and collects, St. Peter's Church, St. Louis, Missouri.

Kelly Fearing: St. Christopher; oil.

Revington Arthur: Last Supper.

Jean Charlot: Fresco; executed at University of Notre Dame, 1955.

Hillis Arnold: Madonna and Child; terra cotta. Church of the Resurrection of Our Lord, St. Louis, Missouri.

Gerald Bonnette: Crucifix of polychromed lead.

Frances Rich: Bronze crucifix.

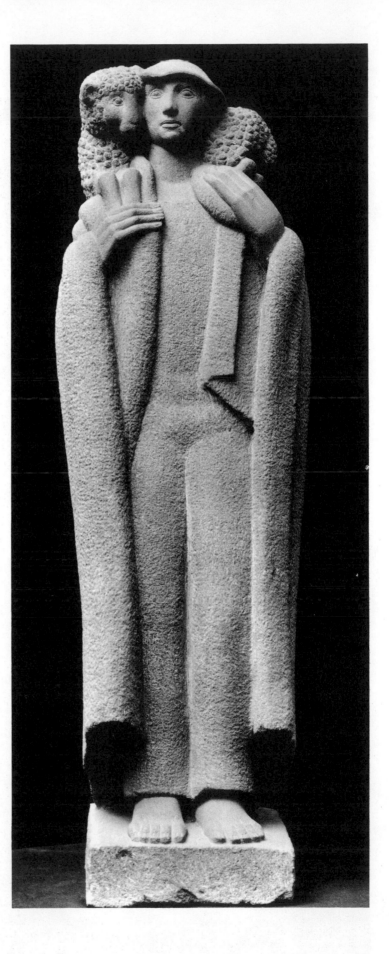

Jean de Marco:
The Good Shepherd; stone.

Janet de Coux:
St. Benedict; stone.

Henry Rox: St. Joan of Arc.

Robert Winthrop White: Madonna and Child; wood.

Hugues Maurin: The Flight into Egypt; polychromed wood.

Frances Rich:
St. Francis of Assisi; bronze.

Charles Umlauf: St. Francis of Assisi.

Jane Wasey: St. Vincent de Paul.

Virgil Cantini: Enamels.

Charles Bartley Jeffery: Translucent enamel on silver cross.

James Kuo: Enamels.

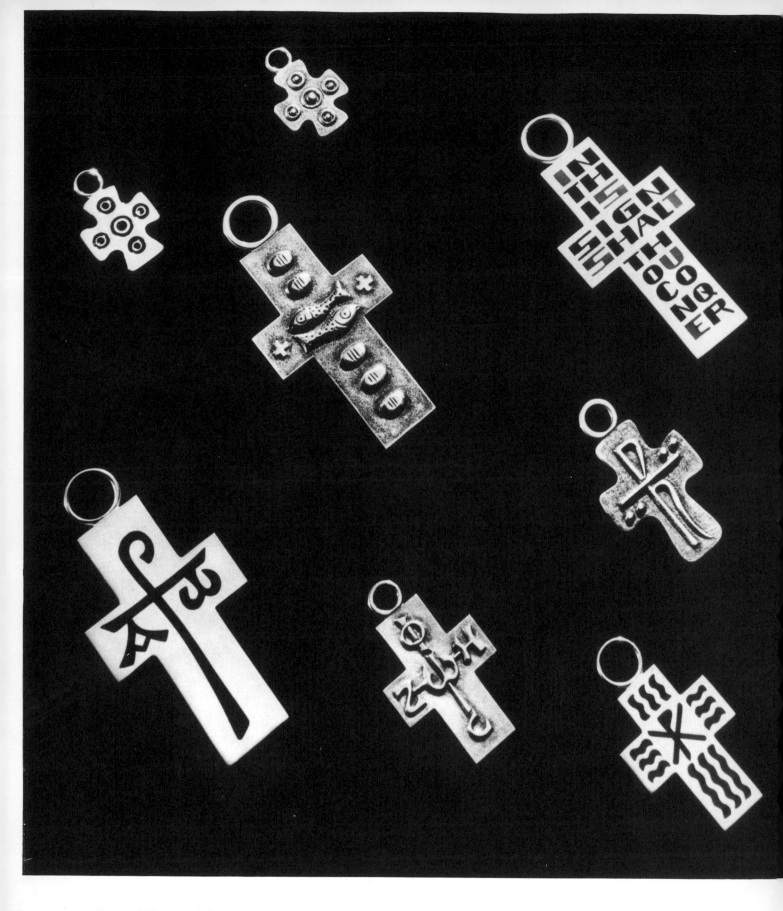

Ilse von Drage: Silver crosses.

Ilse von Drage: Chalice with enameled base.

Ilse von Drage: Silver chalice with engraved base.

Ilse von Drage: Silver chalice with enameled base.

CREDITS

Alber Verlag, Freiburg	p. 73
Benziger Verlag, Einsiedeln	pp. 6, 8
Bogart Studio, New York	p. 116
Photo Anni Borgas, Münster	p. 82
Photo Roger Conant, Burlington, Vermont	p. 111
The Cleveland Museum of Modern Art, Dudley P. Allen Collection	p. 122
Photo Hein Engelskirchen, Hüls b. Krefeld	pp. 41, 48, 55
Gesellschaft für christliche Kunst, Munich	p. 40
Habbel Verlag, Regensburg	pp. 22, 23, 24, 58
Photo Carlfred Halbach, Ratingen	p. 72
Photo Hedrick-Blessing, Chicago	pp. 94, 95, 96, 97
Herder Verlag, Freiburg	pp. 12, 13, 34
Photo Lucien Hervé, Neuilly-sur-Seine, France	p. 17
Galerie Rudolf Hofmann, Hamburg	p. 71
Photo Peter A. Juley & Son	pp. 86, 89, 105, 123
Photo Marburg	p. 69
Photo Frank Lotz Miller, New Orleans	p. 103
Photo Mac Mizuki, St. Louis	p. 110
Photo Judy Lewis Natkin, Chicago	pp. 125, 127
Photo Hans Pillat, Rothenfels	pp. 30, 83
Photo Walter Reuter	p. 26
Photo Reynolds, Photography, Inc., Minneapolis	p. 91
Photo Hugo Schmölz, Cologne	pp. 45, 46, 49, 59
Photo Schwitter, Basel	p. 3
Benn Schnall, New York	p. 100
Schnell & Steiner, Munich	pp. 76, 77, 78, 79
Swiss Consulate, Cologne	p. 9
Photo Viollet	pp. 87, 88
Photo Heinz Vössing, Münster	pp. 43, 74
Werkstätten für Glasmalerei und Mosaik Derix, Kevelaer	p. 82
Photo Raymond C. Wilson, Beaconsfield, England	p. 81

All other photographic material is from the files of Paulus Verlag and the Liturgical Arts Society, New York, or has been kindly supplied by architects and artists.

LOCALITIES

FRANCE   Assy, Audincourt, Montmagny near Paris, Ronchamp, Vence

GERMANY   Aachen, Cologne, Dortmund, Frankfurt, Fulda, Greven, Kleinheubach, Krefeld, Marburg, Marienthal near Wesel, Mülheim, Münster, Norderney, Recklinghausen, Regensburg, Riehl near Cologne, Schweinfurt, Trier, Wesel, Würzburg

SWITZERLAND   Basel, Hirzbrunnen near Basel, Lucerne, Möhlin near Basel, Neubad near Basel, Riehen near Basel, Seebach near Zürich, Zürich

ILLUSTRATIONS PRINTED OPTAK BY EDW. STERN & CO., INC.